Rapture Imminence on Trial

An Examination of the "Any Moment Rapture" of the Church

———

Tom Keeley

Dan,
I hope this book helps you get
excited about our "blessed hope"
Titus 2:13.
God Bless,
Tom

Table of Contents

Diagrams

ACKNOWLEDGMENTS

I want to thank those to whom I personally presented the following material or who attended one of my seminars on the rapture and encouraged me to write a book about it. I have been passionate about this subject from the very beginning of my relationship with Christ. Thanks to the many people who helped me in my walk with Christ and who guided me in how to study God's Word. You were so important in laying a great foundation for me to embark on this project. Thanks to Justus and Heidi who helped with reading and editing the material. Thanks also to Drew for sharing your art skills in working on the cover design and Jason with the diagrams. Thanks to my parents (who are now with the Lord) as they always encouraged me to do my best in academics, athletics, and development of my character. Finally, thanks to the two people with whom I am *one,* who have supported me through many years of my life: my wife, Diane, and my Savior and Lord, Jesus Christ.

INTRODUCTION

Why This Book About Rapture Imminence Matters

There are four popular teachings about the Second Coming of Jesus to rapture the church before what they each understand to be the future wrath of God at the end of the present age. These are the pre, mid, and posttribulation and, more recently, prewrath views. All four can be divided into smaller groups of two. The two classifications we are concerned about here are dependent on whether or not the day of the rapture can be known by Christians awaiting His return. The first group of two, the midtribulation and posttribulation interpretations, allow someone to predict the day of Christ's promised Second Coming to take His followers to heaven. This is because the future ratification of a covenant between Israel and the Antichrist begins the seven years of Daniel's 70th Week, according to Daniel 9:27 (as discussed in detail in Chapter 1). If a person recognizes when this future treaty is made, he or she can count the number of days to either the midpoint or the end of the seven years, thus allowing them to know when the day of a mid- or posttribulation rapture will occur. This creates a contradiction with what Jesus taught when He said:

> "But of that day and hour no one knows…be on the alert, for you do not know which day your Lord is coming…you be ready too; for the Son of Man is coming at an hour when you do not think that He will…the master of that slave will come on a day when he does not expect him and at an hour which he does not know…be on the alert then, for you do not know the day nor the hour." (Matthew 24:36, 42, 44, 50, and 25:13)

Because of these verses, many Bible teachers do not believe the day of the rapture can be predicted. As a result, they reject the mid- and posttribulation positions in favor of one of the other two teachings, the pretribulation or prewrath understanding.

According to the pretribulation teaching, the coming of Jesus to rapture the church could happen *at any moment right now*, without any warning. It is understood to be the next biblical prophecy to be fulfilled in God's prophetic timetable. Thus, it could be called the *present-day, imminent rapture* position. Not being able to know the exact day of Christ's second coming is what has come to be known as *rapture imminence.*

Since the early 1990s, a newer imminent rapture view began to grow in popularity and has taken on the name "prewrath." This teaching arose when some Bible scholars interpreted that certain prophecies need to be fulfilled before the rapture can take place. After they occur *the rapture will become imminent*, but not before then. The two primary authors responsible for publicizing this position are Robert Van Kampen, who wrote *The Sign* in 1992 and *The Rapture Question Answered Plain and Simple* in 1997, and Marvin Rosenthal, who penned *The Pre-Wrath Rapture of the Church* in 1990. The prewrath position does not accept the pretribulation claim that the rapture is presently the next prophecy to be fulfilled, but it does agree that the day of the rapture cannot be known. Prewrath teachers say Christ's coming for the church will become imminent sometime in the future, therefore, it could be labeled the prewrath *future imminent rapture.*

Although the gap between these two rapture scenarios is not great in terms of time, the difference in the events Christians will experience around the time of Christ's second coming, according to each view, is very different. Essentially, it boils down to whether believers alive just before the Second Coming will be raptured before the revelation of the Antichrist and therefore will not undergo his persecution in the form of the great tribulation (pretribulation rapture view) or whether they will be on earth when the Antichrist is revealed and will endure his persecution before being raptured (prewrath rapture view).

One of the leading pretribulation rapture teachers agrees that this is a critical issue and why the correct understanding matters:

> It makes a tremendous difference whether Christ is
> coming now or whether one's prospect is that we will
> go through that tribulation and our only hope of
> seeing Him without dying would be to go through
> that awful time of trouble. — Dr. John Walvoord[1]

I am a firm believer that what a person believes about the future
makes a difference in how they behave in the present. If a person
believes the weather is going to be cold today, they will wear
different clothing than if they are told it will be warm. So it is with
one's understanding of the timing of the rapture. What one believes
makes a difference in how one thinks and feels and will behave
during the current time.

The subject of this book matters because the majority of the church
in the United States believes in the pretribulation rapture scenario,
yet they have possibly never been exposed to any of the problems of
this present-day imminence teaching. The future imminence
understanding of the prewrath rapture may never have been
explained to them since it is relatively new or has possibly been
misrepresented. The belief in the "any moment, right now
possibility of the rapture" is the main pillar that supports the
pretribulation perspective. However, if this pillar doesn't hold up,
then the entire pretribulation rapture position should be doubted and
an alternative position considered.

Logic does not allow us to say that a present-day, imminent rapture
and a future imminent rapture are both true. If one of them is right,
the other must be wrong. It is important that rapture imminence be
properly taught and understood so God's people are not deceived as
we approach the end of this age.

Testing This Trial

Because a large portion of this book follows a trial format, there will
be questions asked concerning the pretribulation rapture teaching of

---

1 *The Day of the Lord*, Dr. John F. Walvoord, Bible.org, February 19, 2019,
https://bible.org/seriespage/5-day-lord (last accessed May 13, 2019).

imminence. Long before the decision was made to write this book, I set out to test the validity of these questions. In order to do this, I presented these questions in personal conversations with some leading pretribulation rapture teachers who often write and speak extensively about their view. In evaluating those discussions, it was easy for me to see the struggle they had in responding to these questions while at the same time maintaining their belief that the rapture has been able to happen at any moment. One of them commented during the course of the dialogue, "These questions are making me think! When are you going to write a book?" It became evident to me that these questions needed to be put into print in order to challenge the pretribulation rapture belief that is so often repeated: *Jesus can come back at any moment.*

Footnote and Endnote Designation

It will be noticed as you read along that there will be many superscript numerals which will designate either footnotes or end of chapter notes. Regular numbers such as 1,2,3, etc. will indicate footnotes at the bottom of the page and they will increase in sequential order for the entirety of the book. Notes at the end of the chapters will use lower case Roman numerals such as i, ii, iii, etc. and they will start over at the beginning of each chapter.

CHAPTER 1

SURVEY OF BIBLICAL ESCHATOLOGY

The Significance of Daniel's 70th Week

One of the key subjects of eschatology is Daniel's 70th Week. This period is part of the broader 70 Weeks prophecy given to the humble prophet Daniel during Israel's captivity in Babylon. The message was delivered by the angel Gabriel, who appeared to Daniel and said:

> "O Daniel, I have now come forth to give you insight with understanding. At the beginning of your supplications, the command was issued and I have come to tell you, for you are highly esteemed; so give heed to the message and gain understanding of the vision" (Dan. 9:22-23).

At the time, the nation of Israel was at a low point in its relationship with God, and the insight given to Daniel was important. God had sternly judged Israel for its rebellion against Him by dispersing them from their place of blessing in the Promised Land. Now they were subjected to the Babylonians and exposed to their false gods. God is about to communicate hope to them concerning the future, but first, He tells them there will be a period of seventy "weeks" of time (in biblical language, a "week" is seven of something, similar to the word "dozen" which means twelve of something). In this context it is best to understand that there will be 70 seven years periods (490 years total) before God's promises would be completely realized.

In this book, I write from the futuristic premillennial perspective. Briefly, this means that God will eventually fulfill His promises to the nation of Israel when Jesus returns in the future to establish a literal kingdom here on the earth. The main reason for this conviction is God's faithfulness to do what He says He will do for Israel in the covenant promises made to them in the Old Testament. His loyalty remains in spite of the unfaithfulness of a majority of the Jewish people throughout their history and, except for a small remnant, their ultimate rejection of Jesus Christ as the Messiah at His first coming.

This important passage continues on:

> "Seventy weeks have been decreed for your people and your holy city to finish the transgression, to make an end to sin, to make atonement for iniquity, to bring in everlasting righteousness, to seal up vision and prophecy, and to anoint the most holy place. So you are to know and discern that from the issuing of a decree to restore and rebuild Jerusalem, until Messiah, the Prince, there will be seven weeks and sixty-two weeks; it will be built again with plaza and moat, even in times of distress. Then after the sixty-two weeks, the Messiah will be cut off and have nothing, and the people of the prince who is to come will destroy the city and the sanctuary. And its end will come with a flood, even to the end there will be war; desolations are determined. And he will make a firm covenant with many for one week, but in the middle of the week he will put a stop to sacrifice and grain offering; and on the wing of abominations will come one who makes desolate, even until a complete destruction, one that is decreed, is poured out on the one who makes desolate" (Dan. 9:24-27).

Premillennialists, regardless of their position on the rapture, are convinced that God is not finished with His plan for Israel.[i] The premillennial view holds that the first 69 weeks (62 weeks + 7 weeks) have been fulfilled, but the final week, commonly called "the 70th Week," is still future. That final seven years will commence with the making of a covenant between "the many" (Israel) and "the prince who is to come" (the Antichrist). The debate about the timing of the rapture focuses on the nature of this 70th Week and God's wrath in relation to it.

A Survey of the Rapture Teachings

There are many different teachings about the second coming of Christ to rapture the church. The following is a list of the four major positions and the primary differences between them, along with three other views on the rapture that influence people's thinking.

1. **Pretribulation**: The rapture can take place at any moment right now. In this view, the entire seven years of Daniel's 70th Week (which they call "the tribulation") is made up of the seals, trumpets, and bowls. Together, these events are considered God's wrath.

2. **Midtribulation**: In this view, the first three-and-one-half years of Daniel's 70th Week is tribulation, but not God's wrath. In midtribulationism, God's wrath is the last three-and-one-half years of the 70th Week, which they call "the great tribulation" because that half becomes more devastating. The rapture occurs at the midpoint.

3. **Posttribulation**: The seven years of Daniel's 70th Week, which posttribulationists also call "the tribulation," are not God's wrath (a view popularized by Robert Gundry), and the church will remain on earth during this time. George Ladd, another well-known posttribulation scholar, differs from Gundry, saying that the tribulation is God's wrath, but God protects the church throughout it. Both agree that the Battle of Armageddon at the end of the seven years is God's wrath and the rapture occurs just before that conflict.

4. **Prewrath**: The rapture occurs at the sixth seal which will be at some unknown time after the abomination of desolation (the midpoint of Daniel's 70th Week). In this view, the first

five seals are tribulation, but not God's wrath. Rather, they are the Antichrist's wrath on anyone for rejecting him. When the seventh seal is removed and the scroll is opened, God's wrath is poured out through angels administering the trumpet and bowl judgments on His enemies on the earth.

There are three other ideas about the Second Coming that, unlike the views above, are not developed systematically from the Bible. They will be acknowledged here, although they will not be considered as possible options to the truth of the Scriptures.

5. **Partial rapture:** In this view, Christians are raptured in stages. Just before the tribulation, faithful disciples will be taken, leaving unfaithful Christians behind. There will be multiple raptures occurring throughout Daniel's 70th Week, occurring successively as Christians repent and become worthy of entering into God's presence.

6. **Pan rapture (indifference):** These people say, "There are other things more important to worry about than the rapture. It will all pan out in the end, so don't worry about it. Let's just keep unity in the body of Christ rather than arguing."

7. **Agnostic:** In this position, you will hear statements like, "There are so many great Christians holding to all the various views. Nobody can really know the correct one." Or, "This is one of those mysteries of God. Perhaps He does not want us to know."

It is helpful to see diagrams of the four most credible and popular teachings about the rapture: pretribulation, midtribulation, posttribulation, and prewrath. One will see that there are many similarities in all of the four views, but there are also significant differences that should not be overlooked. The following charts show the four most common views and include the significant features of each one.[2]

---

[2] For an excellent 15-minute video summarizing the four major views of the rapture, visit https://www.alankurschner.com /2019/02/09/rapture-wrath-ready-or-not-video/.

Pretribulation Rapture

Daniel's 70th week begins with a covenant between Israel and the Antichrist at or near the time of the any moment rapture. This begins the seven years of tribulation which is the seals, trumpets, and bowls and they are considered God's wrath.

Midtribulation Rapture

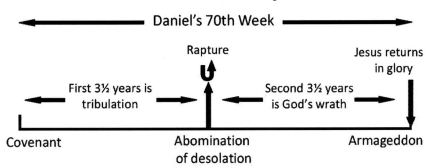

The first 3½ years of the 70th week is tribulation, and not God's wrath. At the midpoint the rapture occurs when Antichrist increases his persecution which is considered God's wrath.

Prewrath Rapture

The church experiences the tribulation under Antichrist which is the first five seals. The rapture becomes imminent at the Abomination of Desolation and occurs at the sixth seal. God's wrath begins then and is described by the trumpets and the bowls.

Posttribulation Rapture

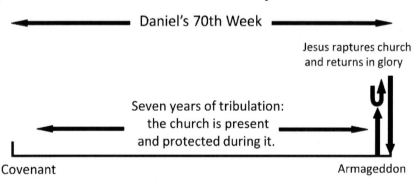

The church is protected through the entire seven years of tribulation and is raptured just before Armageddon which is God's wrath against Antichrist and his followers.

It is significant that all four positions agree that the church will not experience God's wrath, according to 1 Thessalonians 1:10, 5:9: "And [we are] to wait for His Son from heaven, whom He raised from the dead, that is Jesus, who delivers us from the wrath to come...For God has not destined us for wrath, but for obtaining salvation through our Lord Jesus Christ."

However, the most important question concerning the timing of the rapture is, "When does the wrath of God begin?" If the entirety of Daniel's 70th Week is God's wrath, as held by the pretribulation position, then the rapture must occur before that seven-year period begins. Contrary to this, the three other popular positions say there are specific prophesied events within that time period that will take place first. This means the rapture will not be imminent until those prophecies are fulfilled. The prewrath teaching states *the rapture will become imminent later*. It is just not imminent right now. In this, prewrath agrees with the pretribulation teaching that the day the rapture will occur cannot be known.

The proposal of this book is to examine the two rapture teachings that uphold an imminent rapture. It will be argued that the prewrath interpretation of imminence is the better of the two because it stands up to the tests of biblical exegesis, history, and good logical reasoning.

Present-Day Imminence Proclaimed by Pretribulationists

One of the primary goals of this book is to show why the most foundational precept of the pretribulation rapture needs to be questioned. The idea of putting this concept "on trial" is to determine whether the return of Jesus to rapture the church is imminent today. Can it happen right now, at the present time, as pretribulationism contends? Can it occur without any Bible prophecies preceding it to forewarn us? I will begin with the following quotations from leading scholars, theological institutions, and publications that clearly define their understanding of a present-day imminent rapture:

1. Dallas Theological Seminary: "We believe that, according to the Word of God, the next great event in the fulfillment of prophecy will be the coming of the Lord in the air to receive to Himself into heaven both His own who are alive and remain unto His coming, and also all who have fallen asleep in Jesus, and that this event is the blessed hope set before us in the Scripture, and for this we should be constantly looking."[3]

2. Dr. John F. Walvoord, a leading pretribulation rapture scholar and the former president of Dallas Theological Seminary: "Are there predicted events which must occur before the Lord's return? Do the Scriptures present the fulfillment of the hope of His return as an imminent event, i.e., as possible of fulfillment at any moment? …Ever since the Lord Jesus was taken from His disciples to glory on the day of His ascension, the hope of His imminent return has been the constant expectation of each generation of Christians. In the early church this was a dominant theme of the apostles' teaching and an impelling motive in their witness."[4]

3. Dr. Robert L. Thomas, professor emeritus of The Master's Theological Seminary: "Imminence is a crucial teaching of Jesus and the apostles related to end time prophecy. The English word 'imminence' means an event that can occur at any time…There can be no detectable sign that such is about to take place… It is no wonder that the early church and the church throughout the ages has looked for the imminent return of her Lord. He will return with no prior signals to herald His return. Since nothing remains to occur before His coming, it is imminent."[5]

[3]Dallas Theological Seminary doctrinal statement, Article 18, https://www.dts.edu/about/doctrinal-statement/ (last accessed 8/1/2019).

[4] Dr. John F. Walvoord, *The Return of the Lord*, (Grand Rapids, MI: Zondervan, 12th printing, 1978), 48-49.

[5] Dr. Robert L. Thomas, *Evidence for The Rapture,* Dr. John F. Hart, General Editor (Chicago: Moody, 2015), 23,28.

4. Dr. Craig Blaising, professor of theology at Southwest Theological Seminary: "The imminence of the rapture is due to the lack of any signs by which proximity may be determined. It may be near or far. The time is unknown. It will occur unexpectedly. It could happen at any moment."[6]

5. GotQuestions.org, a prominent website promoting the pretribulation rapture: "The word 'imminent' means 'likely to happen at any moment; impending.' When we speak of the imminence of Christ's return, we mean that He could come back at any moment. There is nothing more in biblical prophecy that needs to happen before Jesus comes again."[7]

6. Dr. John MacArthur, chancellor emeritus of The Masters Seminary: "From the very earliest days of the church, the apostles and first-generation Christians nurtured an earnest expectation and fervent hope that Christ might suddenly return at any time to gather His church to heaven… There are no other events that must occur on the prophetic calendar before Christ comes to meet us in the air. He could come at any moment. And it is in that sense that Christ's coming is imminent. In the very same sense, His coming was imminent even in the days of the early church."[8]

7. Dr. Thomas Ice, director of The Pre-Trib Research Center: "That the New Testament teaches Christ could return at any moment is a strong doctrine supporting the pre-trib rapture doctrine. Pretribulationists call this the doctrine of imminence… Imminence in relation to the rapture has been defined as consisting of three elements: the certainty that He

---

[6] Craig Blaising, *Three Views on The Rapture: Pretribulation, Prewrath, Or Posttribulation*, Alan Hultberg, general editor, (Grand Rapids: Zondervan, 2010), 66.

[7] *"Can the Return of Jesus Truly Be Said to Be Imminent?"* https://www.gotquestions.org/imminent-return-Christ.html (last accessed 8/1/2019).

[8] *"Is Christ's Return Imminent?"* Dr. John MacArthur, https://www.gty.org/library/articles/A368/is-christs-return-imminent (last accessed 8/1/2019).

may come at any moment, the uncertainty of the time of that arrival, and the fact that no prophesied event stands between the believer and that hour."[9]

8. Theologian and seminary professor Dr. Charles Ryrie: "If pretribulationism is correct, then the rapture could take place at any time and is clearly imminent… Pretribulationism sees the rapture as the next event on God's program."[10]

9. Dr. David Jeremiah, founder of Turning Point Radio and Television Ministries and senior pastor of Shadow Mountain Community Church: "Without any sign, without any warning, Jesus Christ will return to rapture His saints and take them to heaven. Paul understood the implications of this sign less event. It means we must be ready for the Lord's return at any time and at all times."[11]

10. Dr. J. Dwight Pentecost, author of the well-known eschatological book *Things to Come*: "The doctrine of imminence forbids the participation of the church in any part of the seventieth week… The fact that no signs are given to the church, but she, rather, is commanded to watch for Christ, precludes her participation in the seventieth week."[12]

Observations About Pretribulation Rapture Imminence

We can see three repeated key ideas from these statements:

A. The rapture can happen any moment, right now, at the present time.

---

[9] *"Imminence and the Rapture — Part 1,"* https://www.pre-trib.org/articles/all-articles/message/imminence-and-the-rapture-part-1/read (last accessed 8/1/2019).

[10] Charles C. Ryrie, *What You Should Know About the Rapture* (Chicago, Moody Press, 2nd printing, 1981), 21, 35.

[11] David P. Jeremiah, *Is This the End?* (Nashville: Thomas Nelson, 2016), 247.

[12] J. Dwight Pentecost, *Things to Come* (Grand Rapids: Zondervan, 16th printing, 1978), 204.

B. There are no other Bible prophecies related to the church that must take place before the rapture.

C. This understanding was taught by Jesus and the apostles; it is recorded in the writings of the New Testament; and it continued to be accepted as truth by the early church after the apostles.

These three points will be challenged in this investigation. Recently, I was teaching a Sunday school class on the rapture and did a quick survey concerning attendees' understanding of the subject. It turned out that twenty-two out of the twenty-six said they believed the church would be raptured before the tribulation. Only two thought the church would go into the tribulation and held either mid- or posttribulation positions. The remaining two said they did not know one way or the other. I do not know of an official survey that has been done on this topic, but I would guess that these numbers are fairly typical in the evangelical community.[ii]

After sharing the prewrath interpretation with many people, I found that there is generally a mixed reaction. It is eagerly accepted by some. For others, their belief in an "any moment" rapture prevents them from considering another point of view. Over the years of presenting this position, I began to sense the need to incorporate an apologetic challenge to this understanding of imminence.[iii] That is what this book is about.

By using a question-and-answer format, the ideas put forth by pretribulation theologians will be tested based on their own statements. The questions are mine, and the answers are those given by pretribulation teachers.[iv] I hope that those holding the pretribulation rapture view will give this a fair hearing if for no other reason than that one of its leading proponents in the late 1900s and the early 2000s, Dr. John Walvoord, former president of Dallas Theological Seminary (DTS), opened the door to these questions when he made the following statement:

> The fact is that neither posttribulationism nor pretribulationism is an explicit teaching of Scripture. The Bible does not, in so many words, state either. [13]

This declaration is amazing to me because in my eschatology training at DTS from 1977-1982, no hint of uncertainty regarding the pretribulation rapture position was ever expressed. While Dr. Walvoord never wavered from the position, I began to have some doubts. After graduating from DTS, continued studies over the years about Christ's Second Coming exposed weaknesses in the "any moment" rapture. This was because passages like 2 Thessalonians 1:5-2:9, Matthew 24:3-31, and Revelation 6-7 appeared to point to a non-pretribulational rapture. Finally after forty years of holding to the belief that the rapture could happen at any moment, I became persuaded that the prewrath rapture was the best view. This confidence was strengthened even more after reading a related statement by highly regarded Old Testament scholar Dr. Walter Kaiser[v]:

> The prewrath position is the prophetic position that best understands and properly applies OT [Old Testament] prophecy concerning the Day of the Lord as it relates to the second coming of Christ. If the fathers of dispensationalism had been able to choose between the pretribulation and prewrath views, the prewrath position would have received their vote, hands down. [14]

This comment by Dr. Kaiser is especially meaningful since, as we will discuss, the Day of the Lord is a critical concept related to the truth about the timing of the rapture. Dr. Kaiser implies that the earliest teachers of the pretribulation rapture would not have developed their understanding of rapture imminence had they had a more accurate understanding of Day of the Lord (the Day of the Lord will be studied in detail in Chapter 8). Pretribulation rapture

---

[13] Dr. John Walvoord, *The Rapture Question*, 1st edition, (Findlay, Ohio: Dunham, 1957), 148.

[14] Robert Van Kampen, *The Rapture Question Answered Plain and Simple* (Grand Rapids: Fleming H. Revell, 4th printing, 1999), 198.

literature consistently holds that all seven years of Daniel's 70th Week are God's Day-of-the-Lord wrath. Those holding this view should take Dr. Kaiser's statement to heart and reconsider their understanding of when God's wrath begins.

Summary Up to This Point

Both prewrath and pretribulation teachings say the rapture will be an imminent event because it will occur unexpectedly on an unknown day. Where they disagree is the time that the imminence begins. Pretribulationists say the rapture is *already imminent* since the last prophecy before the rapture has already been fulfilled (the identification of that last prophecy will be considered in great detail in the trial questions). On the other hand, those holding the prewrath view say it will *become imminent* in the future after some necessary prophecies are fulfilled.

There are some pretribulation teachers who think that since prewrath teaches that the rapture will occur after the beginning of the tribulation, a person must be able to know the day it will occur. This is not an accurate understanding of the prewrath view. The prewrath position locates the rapture *at some unknown time* between the midpoint and the end of the seven years of Daniel's 70th Week. This means two things:

1. The last specific prophesied event before the rapture will be the abomination of desolation at the midpoint of the 70th Week (Dan. 9:24-27; 10:31; 12:11-13; Matt. 24:15-22; 29-31).

2. The time the rapture becomes imminent is after the abomination of desolation (2 Thess. 2:1-9).

For more details about this understanding, please read Appendix 3 (page 159: "Imminence Comes After the Abomination of Desolation.")

Why This Trial Format?

Why did I decide to use a "trial" format? I believe it is the clearest, most efficient way of examining the truthfulness of some statement. After changing from the pretribulation to the prewrath position, I would talk to my pretribulation-believing friends by giving the prewrath interpretation of the primary passages dealing with the rapture. I soon realized that most of them were unable to have a meaningful discussion because they could not get past their understanding of present-day imminence. But if this understanding of imminence could be shown to be weak or even incorrect, it opens a whole avenue of discussion that had not been previously possible. That led to the development of a series of questions that reveal problems with the pretribulation understanding of the time of the rapture. I found that challenging the foundational assumptions of pretribulation teachers by comparing them to biblical passages, historical facts, and sound logic, would create greater openness to re-examine the Scriptures to see if they do in fact teach what the prewrath position claims.

All good lawyers carefully choose their questions in attempting to prove their case, and the same thing has been done in this book. There are some lengthy endnotes and appendices that contain more helpful details both to provide clarification of the prewrath view and to assure the reader that, in this format, the pretribulation, imminent rapture position is not being misrepresented. I quote from many individuals and Christian organizations that, on most other doctrines, I would typically agree. I am only challenging their particular theological conclusion that the rapture is presently imminent.

The pretribulation rapture understanding was, for the most part, systematized and became popular as the result of the teachings of John Darby, leader of the Plymouth Brethren movement in Great Britain in the 1830s. In the early 1900s, the position was adopted by C. I. Scofield, who integrated it into the *Scofield Reference Bible*. This allowed the position to propagate quickly until it had become the most popular in the United States by the leading seminaries, Bible colleges, and Christian authors this side of the Atlantic.[vi] However, rapid growth of a teaching doesn't always equate to truth. As believers (especially Bible teachers) discover that a belief we hold is being reasonably challenged, it is our responsibility to search out the scriptures and, if need be, reshape our views. That is what this book is about. There have been many others before me who have switched from a pre-, post- or midtribulation rapture belief to prewrath and then written or spoken about it very well. This book is not going to reinvent the wheel. Rather, it will focus on examining the imminence aspect of the rapture debate in a unique way by asking penetrating questions which test the validity of pretribulation rapture imminence.

^{i} Defining 'Premillennialism'

Premillennialism is the understanding that there are events prophesied in the Bible that are yet to be fulfilled. Primarily, they relate to the promises God made to the nation of Israel in the Abrahamic Covenant (Gen. 12:1-7, 13:14-18, 15:1-21, 17:1-21, 18:10-19) that have not yet come to pass. The focus of the future is on the return of Jesus Christ from heaven to rapture the true believing church into heaven just before the wrath of God begins. This scenario will complete some of the promises God made to Israel in the Old Testament to establish the literal kingdom of God on earth under Christ's rule in Jerusalem. Premillennial Bible teachers understand the key passage of Revelation 20 to depict this literal thousand-year-reign of Christ. It is during this time that Satan will be temporarily confined in the abyss, restricting his influence in the world, so peace, prosperity, and Christ's glory will flourish. Other important passage supporting premillennialism are God's promise of the new covenant to Israel in Jeremiah 31:31-40 and Paul's defense of God's faithfulness to believing Christians who are physical descendants of Abraham, including himself, in Romans 9-11.

^{ii} Defining 'Prewrath'

It has been pointed out that all four of the most popular scholarly teachings on the rapture (pre-, mid-, and posttribulation and prewrath) claim that the rapture happens before the future wrath of God against His enemies on earth (1 Thess. 1:9-10; 5:9). These four rapture positions do not dispute that God will bring literal and cataclysmic destruction on earth as an expression of His anger against sin. They differ as to when that wrath begins. This leads to differences in their beliefs about when the rapture will occur. In the early stages of the development and popularization of the prewrath position by Robert Van Kampen and Marvin Rosenthal, they staked a claim to the identification of their teaching as the "prewrath" rapture. So, even though all four positions teach the principle of the rapture before God's wrathful judgments on earth at the end of this age, only Van Kampen's and Rosenthal's view should be designated as "prewrath" in order to avoid confusion with the other three more traditional teachings.

^{iii} Defining 'Apologetics'

Ever since the early days of my salvation, I have wanted to have good reasons for why I believe as I do. I learned later that this act of defending your beliefs is called *apologetics.* Many books on this subject helped to give answers to questions about what was then my newfound faith. Not wanting to believe in something just because someone says it is true, I felt the need to study and process any new information and come to my own sound conclusions. Even at this early stage of my theological education, I understood the meaning of Peter's command: "Always be prepared to give an answer [*apologia*] to everyone who asks you to give the reason for the hope that you have" (1 Pet. 3:15). This verse is usually understood to mean that Christians are to be ready to present a reasonable defense for their faith before unbelievers. It is also applicable to disagreements between Christians when they have differences in doctrinal beliefs. If they are to be really confident in their positions, they should be familiar with all of the possible views and be able to explain why they believe the one they hold is the best. Then, in brotherly love, they should be able to dialogue and help one another to come to the knowledge of the truth. Note that we see this when Paul and Peter had a significant disagreement about a doctrinal issue related to the gospel in Galatians 2:1-14. They had to have a personal discussion in order to settle the matter.

iv The 'Three Pillars' of the Pretribulation Rapture

In my rapture seminar, I explain how there are three theological "pillars" used to support the pretribulation rapture system. The first and primary one is the present-day, "any moment' imminence of the rapture. The second is the teaching that the entirety of the seven years of Daniel's 70th Week is the Day of the Lord's wrath. The third pillar is the belief that God cannot be working out His plan for the church together with the nation of Israel on the earth at the same time during Daniel's 70th Week. The reason is because they are assumed to be distinct dispensational groups that cannot exist at the same time. The pretribulation rapture position's conclusion is that the church must be removed from the earth before God can fulfill His 70th Week plan for Israel as prophesied in Daniel 9:24-27. For the pretribulation rapture teaching to be correct, all three of these pillars must be true. I present arguments against all three in the seminar, but will focus primarily on the first one, present-day imminence, in this book. The reason being that it supports the entire pretribulation understanding.

v Dr. Kaiser's Quotation: 'The Fathers of Dispensationalism'

Dr. Kaiser is referring to C. I. Scofield, one of the early leading proponents of the pretribulation rapture, as one of these fathers (www.walterckaiserjr.com; see "About Dr. Kaiser," September 14, 2018). But it seems that he was also including John Darby and the Plymouth Brethren who, most scholars agree, first initiated the dispensational pretribulation rapture and influenced Scofield to include that teaching in the *Scofield Reference Bible*. It should also be understood that Dr. Kaiser did speak favorably about the prewrath rapture, but he is not an outspoken promoter of that teaching.

vi History of the Pretribulation Rapture

Throughout most of church history, starting soon after the time of the writing of the New Testament, there was not a great amount of attention devoted to developing a detailed theology of the second coming of Christ. In Great Britain during the 1830s, a strong interest in the subject arose with John Darby and a Christian group he led called the Plymouth Brethren. They became the most influential source of developing and systematizing the teaching of the pretribulation rapture. This opened the door to a greater interest in the subject of biblical eschatology over the past two centuries.

> Undoubtedly, J. N. Darby gave the greatest initial impetus to a systematic pretribulationism as we know it today… In time, he saw the church as a special work of God, distinct from His program for Israel. This truth led him to the position that the

rapture of the church would be before the Tribulation and that
during the Tribulation *God would turn again to deal specially
with Israel.* Those views were accepted and promoted by others.
— Charles C. Ryrie, *What You Should Know About the
Rapture,* 68-69 (emphasis added).

The Plymouth Brethren understood there to be a distinction between God's
dealing with Israel in the Old Testament and the church in the New Testament.
This is what I called in an earlier endnote the "third pillar" that supports
pretribulationism. They concluded that the church must be removed from the earth
by meeting Jesus in the sky in what became known as the rapture. The word
"rapture" is not in any English translation. It is derived from *rapio*, a word in the
Latin Bible to describe the gathering or taking away of the church in 1
Thessalonians 4. Darby and many of the Plymouth Brethren understood its
purpose to be for God to take the church to heaven before He begins fulfilling
Daniel's 70th Week prophecies for Israel. They identified the seven years as "the
tribulation" and equated it with God's end-times wrath before Jesus returns to
earth in power and glory to set up His literal millennial kingdom. There were some
objectors to this understanding within the Plymouth Brethren, led by Greek
scholar Samuel Tregelles, `who became convinced of the posttribulation rapture
position, but the pretribulation rapture theology became more popular as it spread
to North America. Another important player in the growth of this teaching in the
early 1900s was C. I. Scofield, who included it in the notes of his popular *Scofield
Reference Bible.* He accepted the view of Darby and promoted the dispensational
distinction between Israel and the church and the pretribulation rapture scenario,
which made a big impact among Christians in the United States. One leader,
Lewis Sperry Chafer, founded Dallas Theological Seminary in the 1930s and
included the imminent pretribulation rapture in the theology being taught there.
Over the decades, DTS turned out thousands of great Bible teachers who have
gone on to become pastors, missionaries, and professors in many of the top
evangelical seminaries and Bible colleges in the United States and around the
world. Books, songs, seminars, movies, and prophetic teaching ministries
influenced by Dallas Theological Seminary continue to propagate that the rapture
could take place at any moment. The result is that the most popular teaching, by
far, among Bible-believing Christians in the United States is the "any moment"
expectation of the rapture before the presence of the Antichrist and the tribulation.

CHAPTER 2

WHY THEY SAY "IT CAN HAPPEN AT ANY MOMENT NOW"

Although the purpose of this book is not to be a comprehensive critique of every detail of the pretribulation doctrine of imminence, it is helpful to look at the biblical passages used by pretribulation teachers as proof texts and then determine if they can be used to support their position. The following Scriptures and comments are typically used to defend the teaching that the rapture could presently happen at any moment. Let's see what verses are used to promote this doctrine. For simplicity, I use the list provided on The Pre-Trib Research Center website (emphasis added):

- 1 Corinthians 1:7: "*awaiting eagerly* the revelation of our Lord Jesus Christ."

- 1 Corinthians 16:22: "*Maranath*a, *mar* ('Lord'), *ana* ('our'), and *tha* ('come'), meaning 'our Lord, come.' The Arabic greeting implies an eager expectation."

- Philippians 3:20: "For our citizenship is in heaven, from which also we *eagerly wait for* a Savior, the Lord Jesus Christ."

- Philippians 4:5: "The Lord is *near*."

- 1 Thessalonians 1:10: "To *wait for* His Son from heaven."

- 1 Thessalonians 5:6: "So then let us not sleep as others do, but let us *be alert and sober.*"

- 1 Timothy 6:14: "That you keep the commandment without stain or reproach *until the appearing* of our Lord Jesus Christ."

- Titus 2:13: "*Looking for* the blessed hope and the *appearing* of the glory of our great God and Savior, Christ Jesus."

- Hebrews 9:28: "So Christ . . . shall appear a second time for salvation without reference to sin, to those who *eagerly await* Him."

- James 5:7-9: "Be patient, therefore, brethren, until the coming of the Lord. . . for the coming of the Lord *is at hand.* . . behold, the Judge is *standing right at the door.*"

- 1 Peter 1:13: "Fix your *hope* completely on the grace to be brought to you *at the revelation of Jesus Christ.*"

- Jude 21: "*Waiting anxiously* for the mercy of our Lord Jesus Christ to eternal life."

- Revelation 3:11; 22:7, 12, 20: "I am *coming quickly!*"

- Revelation 22:17, 20: "The Spirit and the bride say, 'Come.' And let the one who hears say, 'Come.' He who testifies to these things says, 'Yes, I am *coming quickly.*' Amen. Come, Lord Jesus."

Dr. Thomas Ice summarizes the pretribulation perspective on these verses as follows: "It is significant that all of the above passages relate to the rapture and speak of the Lord's coming as *something that could occur at any moment,* that it is imminent. These passages could only be true if the New Testament is teaching an imminent return."[15] However, when you look closely at all of these verses, *they do not support this premise*. The only clear and certain conclusions we can derive from these verses are as follows:

1. Christ's coming could happen *soon.*
2. We are to be *eagerly and expectantly waiting* for this event.

While many of us, even those not holding the pretrib rapture position, might agree with these two conclusions, pretribulation rapture teachers take this further, beyond what the text itself supports. They go on to make the mistake of claiming that these verses also teach:

3. The rapture can occur *at any moment without any warning.*
4. No other Bible prophecy *needs to be fulfilled before* Jesus comes back.

If you take the time to look carefully at each passage listed above, you will see that conclusions #3 or #4 do not naturally follow. Rather, those two conclusions must be interpreted *into* the biblical text. This is what theologians call *eisegesis*, or identifying meaning that is not actually in the text. Ironically, this is one thing that Dallas Theological Seminary painstakingly attempts to train all of its students to avoid. All of the classes I took were designed to help the students to *exegete* the texts of the Bible, that means to let the text determine the true interpretation out from it. With proper exegesis, we are able to understand the meaning as God and the original authors of the Scriptures intended it, not to import a preconceived explanation into it. Yet ironically, the pretribulation rapture system is the result of *eisegesis* of these passages.

It is interesting to note that Dr. Ice does not include in his list what I refer to as the "big two" passages, which may actually be the

---

15   https://www.pre-trib.org/articles/all-articles/message/imminence-and-the-rapture-part-1, last accessed 8/1/2019.

most often quoted biblical expressions by pretribulationists to support their doctrine of imminence: "He will come like a thief in the night" (Matt. 24:42-44, 1 Thess. 5:2, and 2 Peter 3:10) and "We do not know the day or the hour" (Matt. 24:36, 25:13). Just like all the passages in the Pre-Trib Research Center's list, these passages do not explicitly teach that Jesus can return at any moment right now, either. Nor do they teach that the rapture is the next prophecy to be fulfilled. Once again, those ideas are only there if that meaning is forced into them.[i]

i

---

i **The Passages 'A Thief in the Night' and 'We Do Not Know the Day or the Hour'**

It surprises me that, in his list of key passages on imminence, Dr. Ice does not include two passages from which I often hear two most common pretribulation mantras: "we do not know the day or the hour He will come" (Matt. 24:36, 25:13) and "He will come like a thief in the night" (Matt. 24:42-44; 1-9; 2 Pet. 3:10) used support an "any moment" rapture. Because of this, I felt they should be dealt with in spite of their absence from the list.

Let me give a simple illustration why I believe these verses cannot be used to support the idea that the rapture can come at any moment. When the Major League Baseball season begins early in the spring, *nobody knows the day or the hour* that season will come to its end later in the fall after the last game of the World Series. The finish of the season is not imminent. Even at the end of the regular season and the top teams are qualified, it is getting closer, but the completion of the season is still not imminent. Then after the initial rounds of the playoffs are finished, narrowing it down to the final two teams, still no one knows the day or hour the season will be completely over. In fact, it is possible that even after one or both teams have won two games of the best of seven Series, the day of the end of the season is not imminent. Even though it is near, and fans are eagerly and expectantly awaiting to know who the winners will be, the crowning of the victorious team and the final day of the season is not known, it is still not yet imminent. It is not until one of those last two teams has won three games that the end of the World Series can be said to be imminent since the day of the next game could result with a team winning a fourth game in the Series and the season would finally be over. Whether it's Major League Baseball or the rapture of the church, *not knowing the day or the hour* of a future event cannot be equated to mean that it is imminent and can happen at any moment. Somewhere along the historical line of the development of the pretribulation rapture, someone introduced this false idea of rapture imminence. They incorrectly concluded that the rapture is the next prophecy to happen based on Bible verses that only teach expectation, desire for, or not being too distant away timewise. Teachers continued to present this doctrine without being challenged in their definition of rapture imminence, and it has been assumed to be true from generation to generation.

Next, we will look at the passages containing the expression "he will come like a thief in the night." Once again, these passages do not mean the rapture can happen at any moment for two reasons. First, a closer examination of the contexts of the three occurrences of this expression used by Jesus (Matt. 24:42-44), Paul (1 Thess. 5:1-9), and Peter (2 Pet. 3:10), we see that Christ's return will be like a thief in the night *only to the unbelievers and scoffers* who are not prepared to meet Him. Notice that Paul makes it clear that Christ's return will not be like a thief in the night to alert followers of Christ:

> Now, *brothers and sisters*, about times and dates we do not need to write to you, for you know very well that the day of the Lord will come *like a*

thief in the night. While *people* are saying, "Peace and safety," destruction will come on *them* suddenly, as labor pains on a pregnant woman, and *they* will not escape. *But you, brothers and sisters,* are not in darkness so that this day should surprise you like a thief. *You* are all children of the light and children of the day. *We* do not belong to the night or to the darkness. So then, let *us* not be like *others*, who are asleep, but let *us* be awake and sober (1 Thess. 5:1-6, emphasis mine).

Those who are not spiritually alert enough to recognize the signs of the times will be the ones caught by surprise. His return will not be a surprise to those who are watching and prepared. They are the ones who will see the specific prophecies that Jesus and Paul are clearly teaching about, and *then they will know that His coming is imminent.* Just as with the many other passages Dr. Ice used as proof texts for pretribulation rapture imminence, "the big two" I have dealt with here also fall short of proving the rapture can presently happen at any moment.

CHAPTER 3

THE TRIAL BEGINS – THE OPENING QUESTIONS

We have seen the statements of many of the leading teachers and institutions that claim to substantiate the pretribulation rapture. Before we launch into the first question of this trial, I would like to add one more to that list:

> A fourth argument in favor of the pretribulation rapture is the idea of the doctrine of imminence, meaning that Jesus could come at any time to catch away His church. Other prophetic events may happen after the rapture, *but nothing must happen before the rapture.* It is the next event on God's prophetic calendar. — Dr. Mark Hitchcock[16](emphasis added)

If we consider this definition of imminence, it leads to an interesting question: *If the rapture is the next Bible prophecy to be fulfilled, what was the last prophecy fulfilled before it that now makes the rapture the next in line?* This question arises from my mathematics background since it is similar to a basic arithmetic question: "On a number line, if the *next* number is six, what is the *previous* number

---

16 Dr. Mark Hitchcock, *When Will the Believing Be Leaving: The Truth and Timing of the Rapture* (Dallas: Dallas Theological Seminary, Veritas Series, 2012), 7.

that makes six the next one in line?" Of course, the correct answer is five. Five is the last number that makes six the next one. This exercise in logic was the beginning of what eventually would become an entire series of questions challenging the validity of the belief that the rapture is the next biblical prophecy and that it can happen at any moment, right now.

So let the trial begin.

Setting Forth the Questions

If you are entering into this process with someone holding the pretribulation rapture view (or if you hold this view yourself), it is necessary to start with this preliminary question:

> Do you agree with the pretribulation teaching that the rapture is presently imminent? In other words, do you believe the rapture could happen at any moment, right now, and that it is the next prophecy in the Bible to be fulfilled?

Someone who believes in the pretribulation rapture will answer "yes" to this question. If not, their view is not consistent with the foundation of pretribulation teaching. If they do agree with this statement, this leads to the next question:

> If the imminent rapture is the next prophecy to be fulfilled, *what was the last Bible prophecy fulfilled before it that makes the rapture the next in line?* In other words, at what point in time in past biblical history did the rapture become the next thing prophesied to take place?

Many Christians who believe in the any moment return of Christ may not be able to quickly respond to this question. If so, you can share the following statements from two top pretribulation rapture teachers, Dr. John Walvoord and Dr. Robert Thomas:

> Ever since Jesus was taken up in glory in His ascension, the hope of His imminent return has been the constant expectation of each generation of Christians... In the early church this was the

dominant theme of the apostles' teaching. — Dr. John Walvoord[17]

Imminence is a crucial teaching of Jesus and the apostles related to end time prophecy. — Dr. Robert Thomas[18]

In other words, these two Bible scholars are telling us the apostles believed and taught about an "any moment," imminent rapture after Christ's ascension in about AD 32.

These statements place a spotlight on two points most pretribulation teachers claim: 1) The imminence of the rapture began with the ascension of Christ back to heaven (John 14:2-3; Acts 1:6-11) and 2) the "any moment" rapture teaching originated with (and was taught by) Jesus and the apostles. (I will later discuss two other possible fulfilled prophecies that are also valid answers given by some pretribulationists.)[19]

Now if the person agrees with the statements made by Dr. Walvoord and Dr. Thomas, you can respond:

---

17 Walvoord, *The Return of the Lord*, 42.

18 Dr. Robert Thomas, *Evidence for the Rapture: A Biblical Case for Pretribulationism*, 23.

19 There is a third reasonable answer to the question about the last fulfilled prophecy. It could be the destruction of the temple in Jerusalem in AD 70. This event was originally foreshadowed in Daniel 9:26 and was subsequently predicted by Jesus in Luke 19:43-44 and 21:5-6 in connection to the timing of His second coming. The fulfillment of this prophecy took place when Jerusalem and the temple were destroyed in AD 70, almost forty years after His ascension and prophecies regarding the day of Pentecost were past. If the person says this is the last fulfilled prophecy, there is no disagreement here. It simply means we do not have to go through the following information concerning the prophecies about Peter and Paul. These were all fulfilled somewhere about AD 60-65 during the window of time after AD 32 but before AD 70. So, if the person you are talking to gives the AD 70 answer, then go directly to the questions in Chapter 5 dealing with Jesus' prediction of the destruction of the temple in. But if they have answered with either of the AD 32 prophecies, then continue with what follows here.

Let us consider Christ's ascension in the first
statement. It is obvious that Jesus cannot come for
the second time unless His first coming ends. If that
is so, then the events that ended his first coming were
His death, burial, resurrection, and finally His
ascension back to heaven. In fact, Jesus gave the
prophecy about His ascension at the Last Supper: "If
I go and prepare a place for you, I will come again
and receive you to Myself; that where I am, there you
may be also" (John 14:2-3).

However, it is possible that someone might disagree and say that the
last fulfilled prophecy was the coming of the Holy Spirit at
Pentecost, which happened a few weeks after Christ's ascension. If
so, then respond with the following:

Yes, I agree that the final prophecy before the rapture
is the promise made by Jesus about the coming of the
Holy Spirit in John chapters 14-16. This was fulfilled
on the Day of Pentecost, just a short time after His
ascension. Both of these prophecies were fulfilled
around AD 32, and either one marks a point in time
after which the rapture could have become imminent.

The next question would be:

Would you agree with the pretribulation rapture
teaching that the last prophecy to be fulfilled, thus
making the rapture imminent, was either Christ's
ascension back into heaven or the promise of the
Holy Spirit in about AD 32?

If you receive the answer yes, then proceed by asking the following:

Do you agree with the two pretrib rapture scholars,
Dr. Walvoord and Dr. Thomas, that after the
ascension or the coming of the Holy Spirit, the
apostles understood and taught that Jesus could
return and rapture them at any moment in their
lifetimes?

The expected answer again is yes. It would be good to pause now and summarize what has been agreed upon in accord with pretribulation rapture beliefs:

1. They believe the return of Jesus to rapture the church is presently imminent.

2. They believe that "presently imminent" means it could happen at any moment, right now.

3. They believe no other biblical prophecy needs to occur before the rapture.

4. They believe that either the ascension of Christ to heaven or the coming of the Holy Spirit in AD 32 was the last prophecy that needed to be fulfilled so the rapture is the next one in line.

5. They believe that Jesus and the apostles taught this view of imminence so the rapture could have happened at any moment after the day of Pentecost.

If your friend acknowledges his agreement with these five points, then draw a timeline similar to this one indicating these events.

Pretribulation Prophecy Timeline #1

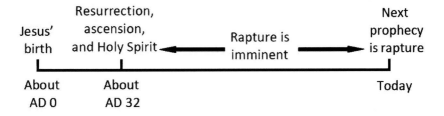

Now ask the following question concerning this diagram:

> Does this timeline represent what you believe to be true about the rapture being the next prophecy, since either Christ's ascension or the coming of the Holy Spirit was the last one that needed to be fulfilled?

If the answer is yes, you can continue.

CHAPTER 4

PROPHECIES ABOUT PETER AND PAUL

Having established that your friend holds to the basic framework of the pretribulation rapture, the trial proceeds. You can now move on to more specific questions about the scriptural support for this position, including whether it's true that there have been no prophecies that need to be fulfilled, from the time of the apostles, before the rapture could occur.

To continue, you can ask your friend if they remember the passage in John 21 where after Jesus' resurrection, Jesus met with Peter and inquired of him three times if he loved Him. Because that story is well known, everyone will probably say yes, so follow that up by asking if they know what was next mentioned in that conversation:

> Do you know what Jesus said immediately after He questions Peter's love and then tells him: "Feed My sheep?"

If they say no, then read John 21:18-19 together (emphasis is mine):

> He said to him, "Truly, truly, I say to you, when you were younger you used to gird yourself and walk wherever you wished, but *when you grow old*, you will stretch out your hands and someone else will gird you and bring you where you do not wish to go."

> Now He said this *signifying by what kind of death* he
> would glorify God.

These two verses open the door for a series of questions that begin
to chip away at the foundation of the pretribulation, imminent
rapture theory. Recall that earlier your friend agreed with the
pretribulation belief that, at the present moment, there are no biblical
prophecies that need to be fulfilled before the rapture will happen.
As the dialog continues, we must make sure to wait for their answer
to each question before moving on to the next one. Remember, we
are using a trial format and there is significance for the specific order
of the questions and the answers which are believed to be true.

> Do you recall that you agreed that the last prophecy
> to be fulfilled before the rapture takes place was
> either Christ's ascension back into heaven or the
> arrival of the Holy Spirit around AD 32?

Wait for their yes answer, then ask:

> Would you also be willing to agree that Jesus is
> clearly giving the young apostle Peter a prophecy
> about his future death as an older man?

It is possible there will be a pause before their answer since this is a
prophecy that many Christians are not familiar with. If there is
hesitation, you can follow up with the following suggestion:

> Let us look at something Peter wrote in 2 Peter 1:13-
> 14 towards the end of his life in about AD 65: "I
> consider it right as long as I am in this earthly
> dwelling, to stir you up by way of reminder, knowing
> that *the laying aside of my earthly dwelling is
> imminent as also our Lord Jesus Christ has made
> clear to me*" (emphasis added).

After they have completed reading these two verses, ask:

> Do these verses, written near the end of Peter's life,
> indicate that Peter understood clearly what Jesus told
> him many years earlier: *that he would die as an older
> man?*

The answer here should be yes. If so, then go to the next question:

> Since Jesus told the young apostle that he would
> experience physical death sometime later as an older
> man, is it reasonable to think that Peter himself
> would have ever believed or communicated to others
> that the rapture could happen at any time while he
> was still alive?

We know that, according to 1 Thessalonians 4:15-17, the rapture is
the catching up of *living Christians before they die*. Since Peter was
told he would die as an older man and wrote about it, *he knew the
rapture was not imminent while he was still living*. Since the other
apostles could not have been teaching contradictory things, they
would not have taught an imminent rapture while Peter was still
living.[i]

Now ask:

> If the rapture were to have happened in Peter's
> lifetime, without him dying in his elder years, what
> would this make Jesus?

The correct answer to this question is: *"He would be a liar or a false
prophet."* Since Jesus cannot be either, it is obvious that Peter's
death had to be fulfilled after Christ's ascension and the Pentecost
experience in AD 32 and before the rapture could happen.

With this in mind, ask the following:

> Since Peter knew that Jesus can only make true
> prophecies, Peter could not have believed or taught
> that the rapture could happen during his lifetime. Do
> you agree with this?

It is probable that they will say, "Yes, that must be true." But if not,
have them explain the contradiction between Peter teaching an
imminent rapture in his lifetime while at the same time knowing that
he had to die as an older man. It is important not to gloss over this
issue. Some pretribulation rapture teachers do attempt to resolve this
problem. Before addressing this, however, I want to show that
Peter's death is not the only prophecy during this period of time that
is problematic for their position.

The next question is:

> Did you know there were also some other prophecies
> made to the apostle Paul that needed to occur in his
> lifetime before he could have been raptured?

This is often a surprise to many believers in the pretribulation rapture. The reason is because teachers of this position are either unfamiliar with these prophecies or, if they are familiar with them, they might ignore them. Have your friend read the following passages and see if they agree with the stated observations and conclusions:

> Coming over to us, he took Paul's belt, tied his own
> hands and feet with it and said, "The Holy Spirit says,
> 'In this way the Jewish leaders in Jerusalem will bind
> the owner of this belt and will hand him over to the
> Gentiles'" (Acts 21:11, NIV).

This is a prophecy made by a prophet named Agabus, through the Holy Spirit, while Paul is in Caesarea. If Paul will be bound by the Jews and delivered to the Gentiles sometime in the future after he arrives in Jerusalem, then the rapture *cannot be imminent at that time either.* The rapture cannot happen until after Paul arrives in Jerusalem and is taken captive. Otherwise, the Holy Spirit would be inspiring a false prophecy. After Paul arrives in Jerusalem, sure enough he is taken captive and has the following experience:

> The following night the Lord stood near Paul and
> said, "Take courage! As you have testified about me
> in Jerusalem, so *you must also testify in Rome*" (Acts
> 23:11, NIV, emphasis added).

This is another prophecy that must be fulfilled before the rapture can occur. This passage clearly states that Paul must be a witness for Jesus in Rome. Thus, the rapture *cannot happen until Paul completes the long trip to Italy and testifies for Jesus in Rome.* Otherwise, Jesus would be a false prophet. About two years later while on the boat headed to Rome a storm arises resulting in the next supernatural encounter the apostle has:

> Last night an angel of the God to whom I belong and
> whom I serve stood beside me and said, "Do not be
> afraid, Paul. *You must stand trial before Caesar*; and

> God has graciously given you the lives of all who sail
> with you" (Acts 27:23-24, NIV, emphasis added).

In the midst of a shipwreck, an angel appears and assures Paul that
he will not die because he has to appear before Caesar. In other
words, the rapture cannot be imminent until sometime after Paul
meets with Caesar in Rome. Otherwise, the angel would have been
making a false prophecy.

The conclusion? The rapture could not have happened at any time
during these years because these prophecies made about Paul
needed to be fulfilled. Otherwise, the Holy Spirit, Jesus, and the
angel were false prophets. This leads to the next question:

> Based on these prophecies, would you agree that an
> "any moment, imminent" rapture during the lifetimes
> of Peter and Paul cannot be true?

The answer can be none other than yes. So, we have prophecies
made about the lives of two of Christ's apostles that directly
contradict the understanding that the rapture became imminent right
after AD 32 and was taught by the apostles. This directly
undermines proof texts by pretribulationists that support an "any
moment" rapture (see Chapter 2).

This point cannot be over-emphasized. Recall that I showed
quotations by two leading pretribulation rapture scholars claiming
that present imminence was a crucial teaching and a dominant theme
of the apostle's teaching. Yet both Peter and Paul knew that there
were personal and detailed prophecies made about them that would
prohibit the rapture from taking place at any moment while they
were still alive. Thus, the apostles could not have taught, either
verbally or in writing, that the rapture of the church could happen at
any moment *until after these prophecies were fulfilled.*

At this point, the following question can be raised:

> Does this information make you wonder whether the
> pretribulation rapture teachers are aware of these
> problems with their teaching of imminence? And if
> so, have they made any attempt to respond to them?

The answer to the first question should be yes, along with the answer to the second question, which is also yes. There has been an attempt by some pretribulation teachers to deal with this problem, so let's look at one scholar's response (emphasis added):

> As far as *the church at large* was concerned, the information to Paul and Peter *did not deter their belief in imminence* because on a given day few would know whether Paul or Peter was still alive, and most of them were not informed about the predictions.[20]

My response to this statement is: "Time out! Where did this 'church at large' get their belief that the rapture was imminent as Dr. Walvoord claims?" We can safely say that the early church's sources were not Peter or Paul. These two apostles could never have taught that the rapture was imminent during their lifetimes because they knew the prophecies about their lives had to be fulfilled first. It is almost certain that the other apostles working alongside Peter in Jerusalem and Palestine would have known of the prophecy Jesus made about his death. We know that the apostle John knew because he is the one who recorded the conversation in his gospel. The rest of the twelve apostles also had met with Paul, and we can be assured that they were all in agreement with their understanding about the timing of the Second Coming. It is only logical that none of the apostles would have taught about an "any moment" rapture that was the next prophecy to be fulfilled. Thinking that the universal church had a belief in imminence is an assumption with no biblical or rational basis.

The Scriptures clearly contradict the pretribulationist's belief that the apostles taught that the rapture was imminent at that time. This is a major crack in the pillar of pretribulation rapture teaching. If the apostles could not have taught that the next prophecy to be fulfilled was the rapture, then what could possibly be the source of that theological position? Could it be that it became an assumption originating in the minds of the early teachers of the pretribulation rapture centuries later in the mid-1800s and early 1900s? (see p. 18)

---

[20] John F. Walvoord, *The Blessed Hope and the Tribulation* (Grand Rapids: Zondervan, 1976), 73.

ⁱ **Ryrie's Comment about Jesus' Prophecy of Peter's Death**

It is ironic that one prominent pretribulation imminence rapture teacher labels the comment by Jesus about Peter's death in John 21:18-19 as a prophecy (that, as an older man, Peter would die as a martyr):

> John 21:18-19; Ryrie states that this passage is a prophecy of the martyrdom of Peter. (Footnote from *The Ryrie Study Bible, New American Standard Translation* (Chicago: Moody Press, 1978 edition), 1642.

The same scholar goes on to comment on what Peter wrote in 2 Peter 1:14 about his own death:

> 2 Peter 1:14; the laying aside of my earthly dwelling. Because of Christ's prediction (John 21:18), Peter knew that he would soon die. (Footnote from *The Ryrie Study Bible*, 1873).

Anyone who claims that the apostles taught that Jesus could return to rapture the church at any moment while Peter was still alive is contradicting one of their own leading scholars as well as Jesus. Dr. Ryrie is correct in his comments about these two passages in the *Ryrie Study Bible*, but he is contradicting himself if he believes the rapture could happen in the lifetimes of the apostles.

CHAPTER 5

ONE MORE FIRST CENTURY PROPHECY

At this point of the trial, a present-day imminent rapture believer might say: "I may have been wrong about the AD 32 date, but the rapture must have become imminent once the prophecies concerning the lives of Paul and Peter were fulfilled around AD 65." Your response should include the following statement and diagram:

> Now that we know that the rapture could not have been imminent around AD 32, we must change the timeline to show the possibility of imminence beginning after AD 65. We now have a new diagram:

Pretribulation Prophecy Timeline #2

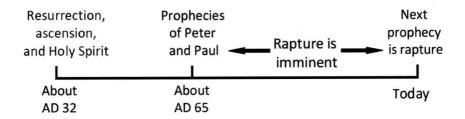

This question now follows:

> Since the rapture could not have happened during the
> lifetimes of Paul and Peter, are there any prophesied
> events after AD 65 that would have to be fulfilled
> before it did become imminent?

The answer to this question is yes, but in case it is not known by the person you are talking to, you might give them a hint by reading Daniel 9:26: "Then after the sixty-two weeks the Messiah will be cut off and have nothing, and the people of the prince who is to come *will destroy the city and the sanctuary*" (emphasis added).

This prophecy by Daniel is referenced by Jesus about six hundred years after it was written, just days before He was taken to be crucified. After an intense rebuke of the Jewish religious leaders in the temple (Matthew 23), Jesus and His apostles were departing from that holy place of worship. His disciples were in awe of the magnificence of the structures that made up the temple complex as they walked away and headed toward the Mount of Olives. Matthew records the Lord's response (emphasis added):

> Jesus came out from the temple and was going away
> when His disciples came up to point out the temple
> buildings to Him. And He answered and said to them,
> "Do you not see all these things? Truly I say to you,
> not one stone here shall be left upon another, *which
> will not be torn down.*" (Matt. 24:1-2)

No matter which rapture position one holds, everyone agrees this prediction is referring to the destruction of the temple and ultimately most of Jerusalem in AD 70. This prophecy, recorded both by Daniel and the Lord Jesus Himself, needed to be fulfilled before the rapture could be the next prophecy to be fulfilled. *The rapture could not be imminent as long as the temple was standing.*[i] This forces the pretribulationist to continue to push forward the date of an imminent rapture. Based on the prophecies about Jesus and the Holy Spirit, it could not be imminent until after AD 32. Based on the prophecies to Peter and Paul, it could not be imminent until after about AD 65. Now, based on the prophecy regarding the temple, another diagram shows the new consideration about rapture imminence:

Pretribulation Prophecy Timeline #3

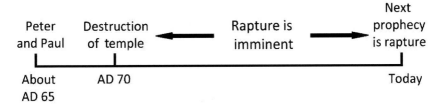

If the reasoning up to this point is valid, the next few questions will be very problematic for the person who holds to the pretribulation rapture. The first one is this:

> What happened to the nation of Israel after Jerusalem and the temple were both destroyed in AD 70?

The answer is known by most who are familiar with Jewish history: Israel was dispersed all over the world, or as some would say, it was the beginning of the Diaspora. The Hebrew people were scattered, resulting in the loss of their homeland and therefore their identity as a sovereign nation. Not only were they no longer in the land God had promised them, but they had no recognizable national political or religious leadership. This presents one more difficulty for the pretribulation rapture. According to this position, the "any moment" rapture will take place at the same time (or near to the same time) the nation of Israel signs a covenant with the future Antichrist. This event initiates the 70th and final week of Daniel's prophecy: "And he [Antichrist] will make a firm covenant with the many [national Israel] for one week" (Dan. 9:27).[21] How can this happen if there is no nation of Israel with which to make such a treaty? It can't!

This dilemma raises the next three questions:

> Are you aware that most pretribulation rapture teachers say the "any moment" rapture and the

---

21 Dwight Pentecost expressed this position when he wrote: "It is evident from Daniel 9:27 that the 70th Week begins with a covenant that is made with many for one week, or seven years." [J. Dwight Pentecost, *Things to Come* (Grand Rapids: Zondervan, sixteenth printing, 1978), 249].

making of a covenant between the Antichrist and Israel will take place at or about the same time? [22]

After a response of either yes or no, present the following question:

If Israel was not a sovereign political nation in their promised land after AD 70, is it possible for there to have been a signing of a covenant between Israel and the Antichrist while under these conditions?

The answer to that question is no. This leads to the third question:

If the prophecy of Daniel's 70th Week cannot happen without the existence of a sovereign nation of Israel, could the rapture have taken place at any moment once Israel was dispersed in AD 70?

Once again, the correct answer to this last question is no. A covenant between the nation of Israel and the Antichrist would have been impossible during the time Israel did not exist as a sovereign nation. Therefore, during that time, Daniel's 70th Week could not begin. If it could not begin, the rapture could not occur. It was not until the Jews re-gathered into their land and were recognized as a sovereign political state that they could sign this treaty and commence the final week of Daniel's prophecy. This begins what the pretribulationists claim is God's Day-of-the-Lord wrath. It is this from which they also say the imminent rapture saves the church. Therefore, *the rapture was not imminent during the entire time of Israel's dispersion.* This is no small problem for the pretribulation rapture position.

In light of these conditions, a thinking person would be led to the next question:

When did it become possible for Israel, as a nation, to sign a covenant and fulfill the prophecy in Daniel 9:27 and thus allow for the rapture to occur?

Most students of premillennial eschatology see the best answer to

---

22 One way the pretribulation rapture teachers try to get around this issue is to create a gap of time between the rapture and the signing of the covenant. For more on this, see Appendix 6, page 177.

this as 1948. It was by then that the Jewish people had reacquired much of their previously lost land and had worked diligently over many years to be recognized internationally as an independent, sovereign nation.[23]

It should also be taken into consideration that Israel did not officially regain control of their capital city, Jerusalem, until 1967. This is a significant piece of the eschatological puzzle as we recall the words of the angel Gabriel about the 70 Weeks prophecy:

> Seventy weeks have been decreed for your people *and your holy city*... So, you are to know and discern that from the issuing of a decree to restore and rebuild Jerusalem... and the people of the prince to come will destroy *the city* and the sanctuary (Dan. 9:24-26, emphasis added).

Once more, we must adjust the rapture imminence timeline. Only this time, it is not by a few years or decades, but rather by an incredible 1900 years, from AD 70 until 1967. The fulfillment of Daniel's prophecy is required in order to allow for the hope of the rapture to occur at any time.

Let's look at yet another new timeline:

Pretribulation Prophecy Timeline #4

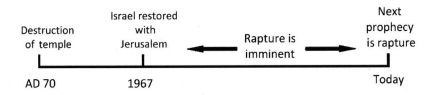

Perhaps you might be wondering whether pretribulation scholars

---

23 I highly recommend watching the DVD *"The Hope: The Rebirth of Israel"* produced in 2015 by The Christian Broadcast Network. This traces the historical struggle of the Jewish people and the Zionist movement for the fifty years prior to their officially becoming a nation again in 1948.

have taken this problem into consideration. Yes, they have. Here is how two teachers address this point (emphasis added).

The first is as follows:

> The precise world conditions immediately after the coming of the Lord for the church anticipated that Israel would be in Palestine in sufficient numbers to be a recognizable political entity. With them the world leader would form a covenant... Before World War I this would have been *almost impossible*, and prior to World War II this would have been *improbable*. But the formation of the state of Israel and the influx of pilgrims make the *plausibility* of such a covenant evident to anyone.[24]

And the second:

> I think that before Israel was born as a nation that there was *nothing really relevant* to the second coming of Christ. Because *that had to be in place* before the rest of the pattern would be *meaningful* ...Since the *restoration of Israel* as a state and the recapture of old Jerusalem, I believe the pattern is really coming together rapidly.[25]

At this point, I must once again shout: "Time out! Stop right here!" Both of these statements are clear contradictions to statements about an "any moment," imminent rapture. Previously, Dr. Walvoord stated that the rapture has been possible at any moment since the time of the apostles. But here, he says the Second Coming and the rapture were "almost impossible" and "improbable" or "not really relevant" until the restoration of Israel in 1948 and the regaining of control of Jerusalem in 1967. Both of these statements cannot be true at the same time.

Since this is a trial on a theological conclusion based on the Word of God, a teaching must be accountable to historical facts, logical

---

24 Dr. John F. Walvoord, *The Return of the Lord*, 16.

25 Hal Lindsay, *"Eternity"* magazine, January 1977, 19.

consistency, and good Bible interpretation. Yet, there are obvious errors in their teaching:

1. They are mistaken in believing the rapture has been imminent since AD 32 (Christ's ascension or the coming of the Holy Spirit).

2. They are mistaken in believing the rapture has been imminent since AD 65 (prophecies about Peter and Paul).

3. They are mistaken in believing the rapture has been imminent since AD 70 (the dispersion of Israel after the destruction of Jerusalem and the temple).

4. They are mistaken in believing the rapture was imminent before the fulfillment of the re-establishment of the nation of Israel (therefore making it possible for Israel to sign a covenant with the Antichrist) and the retaking of Jerusalem in 1967.

Now, the question to be dealt with is this: Has the rapture been imminent since 1967?

ⁱ **About Temple Destruction and Imminence**

Dr. John F. Walvoord maintains that the prophecy about the destruction of the temple, made by Jesus in about AD 32 and fulfilled in AD 70, was not required to be fulfilled *before* the rapture. He contends that the teaching of rapture imminence is not affected by this prophecy. It could have happened *before or after* the fulfillment. Let us look at his statement (emphasis added):

> Some of the events predicted were not clearly related to the rapture such as the destruction of Jerusalem in AD 70; at the time of its prediction this event *could have either preceded or followed the rapture.* Fulfillment, however has indicated that it would precede the rapture. (*The Blessed Hope and the Tribulation,* 1976, 71)

I will present the argument against rapture imminence *after* the temple's destruction in AD 70 in the main body of the chapter. I have included this endnote because it is necessary to deal with Dr. Walvoord's statement that the rapture could have happened *before* the destruction of the temple. Although it is a moot point now that the prophecy has been fulfilled, I still want to show that the rapture was not possible between Peter's death (about AD 65) and the time the temple was destroyed in AD 70. Contrary to Dr. Walvoord's statement, the rapture could not have been imminent for those five years because of events that the Bible says will take place in the 70th Week of Daniel. During those final seven years, *it is necessary for a temple to exist* in light of two biblical prophecies that link it to the Antichrist. First, we are told that the Antichrist will stop temple sacrifices (Dan. 8:9-13; 9:27, 12:11; Matt. 24:15). Second, we are told that the Antichrist will enter the temple of God and demand that the world worship him as God (2 Thess. 2:1-4).

We know that Jesus predicted the temple's destruction, but the activities of the Antichrist during the tribulation are done in the context of a functioning temple. It is unlikely that Christ's prophecy of the tearing down of the temple that existed during His lifetime could have taken place after an "any moment" rapture and the signing of the covenant, which teachers of the pretribulation rapture say begins Daniel's 70th Week. This would mean that *in just three-and-one-half years after the covenant signing, the temple of Jesus' day would have had to be destroyed and another one built to replace it.* Recall that halfway through the 70th Week, the Antichrist must enter a temple and fulfill the two things just mentioned above.

For this scenario to be possible, two major problems must be dealt with. First is the physical ability back in those days to tear down that magnificent temple building complex, then reconstruct something like it in that short amount of time. Second is the political relationship between Rome and Israel. Since the Roman emperor would have been the only one qualified to fulfill these prophecies about the Antichrist, the following would have to take place: Caesar would have had to sign a treaty with Israel, then turn around and destroy their temple, then rebuild it and allow their worship to resume, then just a short time later, enter it, stop the sacrifices, and demand that everyone worship him as God. All of this would have had to take place in just 1260 days. This is what Dr. Walvoord is telling everyone to believe if the "any moment" rapture were to happen before the temple's destruction.

I am challenging Dr. Walvoord's reasoning and any other pretribulationist to explain how the rapture could be possible at any moment before the prophecy of the temple's destruction was fulfilled in AD 70. This makes the feasibility of the rest of the prophetic events of first half of Daniel's 70th Week in the historical context of the first century totally unbelievable. Since it has already been shown that the rapture could not have happened before the death of Peter and the events in Paul's life in AD 65, we now see that this rejection of an "any moment" rapture must be extended until after AD 70 when the temple was destroyed.

CHAPTER 6

THE PROBLEM WITH IMMINENCE SINCE 1967

Let's quickly review where we are at this point. In the previous chapters, we looked at some of the Bible prophecies that appear to be unknown to pretribulation rapture believers since they clearly contradict the claim that the rapture has been the next prophecy to be fulfilled since the time of the apostles. Their position has been challenged by posttribulation scholars, and more recently by prewrath teachers, who have argued against this teaching.[26]

We examined how some pretribulation rapture teachers have made the inaccurate claim that the rapture became imminent around AD 32, after Christ's ascension or the arrival of the Holy Spirit on Pentecost. It was shown that there were clear prophecies about the lives of the apostles Paul and Peter that had to be fulfilled before the rapture of the church could take place. The necessity of these

---

[26] Three examples of such teachers are: 1) Posttribulation teacher Robert Gundry (see *The Church and the Tribulation* (Grand Rapids: Zondervan, 5th printing, 1980), 37-40, 42); Prewrath teacher Marv Rosenthal (see *"Imminence: Does the Bible Teach an Any Moment Rapture?" Zion's Fire Magazine*, August/September 1990; and 3) Prewrath teacher Ron Wallace, YouTube video: *"The Prewrath Rapture: Imminence,"* from the "Speaking the Truth in Love" conference at Grace Community Church in Auburn, Washington; July 12, 2011.

prophecies being fulfilled moved the potential time frame of the rapture up to about AD 65. Other pretrib teachers understand the last prophecy to be fulfilled before the rapture to be the destruction of the temple, which took place in AD 70. However, because this monumental event resulted in the dispersion of Israel from their land and the loss of their national identity, this pushed the date of the imminent rapture back even further. Without being an official nation, Israel would have been unable to sign a covenant with Antichrist to kick off the seven years of Daniel's 70th Week.[27] This pushed the date of an imminent rapture back to 1948 when Israel once again became a sovereign nation or 1967 when it regained control of its capital city, Jerusalem.

Pretribulationists have been proclaiming that the "any moment" rapture will take place at approximately the same time as the treaty signing since they believe the entirety of those seven years is God's wrath and the church must be taken before that comes upon the world. Without Israel's national restoration and control of their Promised Land and capital city, this prophecy could not be fulfilled. If the rapture could not be imminent over those 1900 years, this brings us to the point of considering whether the rapture has been imminent since 1967.

I am going to propose that another reason for doubting an "any moment" rapture over this period of time is how *illogical* it is to believe that the rapture could occur suddenly at any moment today, then be followed immediately by the prophesied events during the first three-and-one-half years after it. We are now going to examine

---

[27] For a typical explanation of a "week" meaning a period of seven years, see *Daniel's Prophecy of the Seventy Weeks* by Alva J. McClain (Winona Lake: BMH Books), 12-15. Also, Dr. J. Dwight Pentecost agrees with McClain when he wrote: "Daniel was first informed that God's program would be consummate in 70 'sevens.' Since Daniel had been thinking of God's program in terms of years (v. 1; cf. Jer. 25:11-12; 2 Chron 36:21), it would be most natural for him to understand these 'sevens' as years. Whereas people today think in units of tens (e.g., decades), Daniel's people thought in terms of 'sevens' (heptads). Seven days are in one week... seventy 'sevens,' then is a span of 490 years." (J Dwight Pentecost, commentary on Daniel in *The Bible Knowledge Commentary of the Old Testament* Wheaton: Victor Books, 1985), 1361.

the feasibility of whether those events could commence immediately and be fulfilled in just 42 months after the rapture and a treaty signing. To do this, we will compare the conditions that have existed in the world from 1967 up to the present time. Then we will ask this question:

> Is it reasonable for the political, economic, and spiritual conditions predicted in the first half of Daniel's 70th Week to have occurred from 1967 up to this very moment?

If it can be shown that those prophesied events are highly improbable, then pretribulationism has another strike against it. There may be some who object to the appeal of common sense here.[i] However, the tool of common sense is found in almost every area of life in determining what is true, whether it is history, rocket science, legal judgments, or Bible interpretation. In this, I am in good company with one of my seminary professors and one of the leading defenders of the pretribulation rapture, Dr. Charles Ryrie. Although he would disagree with me about the timing of the rapture, he agrees with me on the importance of common sense. In his book, *What You Should Know About the Rapture,* he calls it "sound reasoning":

> One can hold to any interpretation one wishes. The question is not, "Is it *possible* to interpret that way?" The question is, "Is it *reasonable* to do so?" … Any explanation is possible, but is it the most likely meaning of the text?[28]

At the time of this statement, Dr. Ryrie was appealing to the use of sound reasoning to determine the best interpretation when comparing pretribulationism to posttribulationism. This was about ten years before the prewrath teaching was introduced. If that great theologian could appeal to the use of good logic to determine what he considered the correct view at that time, the same thing should be permitted now. The difference is that this time, common sense reasoning will result in disqualifying the pretribulation view and supporting the prewrath position.

---

[28] Charles Ryrie, *What You Should Know About the Rapture*, 81.

Are the 70th Week Events Reasonably Possible in Recent Times?

To answer this question, let us summarize the events that all rapture teachers agree will take place in the first half of the seven years of Daniel's 70th Week prophecy.

1. There will appear in the Middle East an Antichrist person who is a spiritual, military, and political leader (Dan. 7:23-26; 8:23-25).

2. This Antichrist will be in the position where he can make a covenant with Israel, which initiates the 70th and final week, or seven years, of Daniel's prophecy (Dan. 9:26-27).

3. This Antichrist and his worldwide comrades will go from a regional power to global authority over military, political, economic, and spiritual control in just three-and-one-half years.

   a. The Antichrist will survive a mortal wound, possibly even being raised from the dead (Rev. 13:3-14).

   b. The Antichrist's partner, the false prophet, will produce other convincing miracles, deceiving most people and pointing them to give allegiance to this new world dictator (Rev. 13:11-17).

   c. The Antichrist will enter a Jewish holy place three-and-one-half years after the signing of a covenant and stop their sacrifice worship system (Dan. 8:9-13; 9:27; 12:11).

   d. The Antichrist will demand that the world submit to his authority and worship him as God (2 Thess. 2:3-4).

   e. The Antichrist will begin universal persecution against any who refuse to take his mark (Matt. 24:15-22; Rev. 13:5-8).

My next two questions in the trial are based on the three main points #1 through #3 above:

> Do you agree that the events described will take place in the world during the first half of Daniel's

70th Week as the Antichrist rises to his position of dominance on the international scene?

After the probable affirmative answer, follow it up with the next question:

Do you agree with the pretribulation imminent rapture view that it is reasonable that all of these events could have begun and been completely fulfilled in three-and-one-half years, at any moment, from 1967 even up to this very present time?

The answers to the second questions must be yes if they believe the rapture has been, and still is, presently imminent. This being the case, we must now closely examine the possibility of whether these future historical prophecies could reasonably have occurred from 1967 until the present time. Because the imminence scenario has been accepted by millions of Bible-believing Christians, the following questions may be unchartered waters for many. Let us begin with the first one:

Have you ever been shown any reasons to doubt the possibility of an "any moment" pretribulation rapture happening since 1967, even until today?

More than likely, they will answer no. So, then ask:

Would you be willing to consider that between 1967 and now it has been improbable for the things the Bible says will happen in the first half of Daniel's 70th Week to have begun to take place at any moment and be completed in three-and-one-half years?

If they agree to this, then you can propose the following statement, and then ask them about the information that follows:

I am about to present some reasons for why it is illogical to believe that an "any moment" rapture could have occurred, and then be followed immediately by all the events of the first half of the tribulation, since 1967.

It is acknowledged that this is a bold claim because it cuts against the grain of many leading Bible teachers in the evangelical church over the past few generations. But this challenge must be heard if one is seeking to decide whether what they have heard from these teachers is true, especially in light of the prewrath interpretation to which many pre- and posttribulation rapture teachers are turning. It must not be dismissed simply because it does not agree with one's tradition.[29]

The following section is an extended monologue that deals with the prophecies related to the first half of Daniel's 70th Week. It will be followed by a few more questions as the trial continues. The issue under consideration is how *reasonable* it is to believe that the events of the first three-and-one-half years after the rapture could possibly happen immediately, in light of the present world conditions. The pretribulation position is forced to say that *they must be able to actually take place in the next three-and-one-half years* from right now if the rapture is, in fact, presently imminent. I will contend that this is unreasonable when examined closely. Instead, the argument will be put forward that the prewrath scenario is not only more logical, but also fits better with the plain teaching of the Bible.

Let us look at the following line of reasoning:

The main concept revealed in Daniel's 70th Week prophecy concerns the most famous person who will have ever lived other

---

[29] There is a parallel here with the Sermon on the Mount in Matthew 5-7, where Jesus confronted many traditional teachings and practices of the Jews at that time. Those practices needed to be corrected so the people could have the proper interpretation rather than continuing man's failed attempts to properly interpret God's Word over the centuries. Remember how Jesus repeated many times: "You have heard," followed by His statement of their traditional belief. Once He had stated their traditional belief, He then responded, "But I say," followed by God's intended meaning that they had missed. The goal of prewrath rapture teachers is to do the same thing here, to correct the half-truths about the timing of the glorious return of Jesus before God's wrath. Of the four possibilities, AD 32, 65, 70, or 1967, the specific date depends on which prophecy a pretribulationist accepts as the last one fulfilled, making the imminent rapture the next in line. These different options were dealt with earlier in detail as the trial progressed. The age group of the unrevealed Antichrist must be designated as an adult because, at the time of the fulfillment of the prophecy, he will be in a position of international leadership. It is improbable that a child or teenager or a frail, elderly person would be the one to make a covenant with Israel and then, in just three-and-one-half years later, be able to enter the Jewish temple and demand to be worshipped as God.

than Jesus Christ. Daniel describes him as "the prince who is to come," and he is elsewhere named "Antichrist," "the beast," or "the man of sin" (Dan. 9:26-27, 11:36-45; 2 Thess. 2:3-4; 1 John 2:18; Rev. 13:1-8).

Both the Old and New Testaments, along with the writings of the ancient church fathers, (see Appendix 4, page 163) bear witness that the activities centered around this individual will result in the most horrific conditions in the history of mankind. It has been shown that the pretribulation rapture requires that those events have had the potential to begin at any moment from 1967 until today. Those worldwide incidences are depicted by Daniel in his writings, by Jesus in the Olivet Discourse, by Paul in his Thessalonian epistles, and by John in the Revelation. But there are good reasons to doubt that these specific biblical prophecies could possibly begin to take place at any moment since 1967 and be fulfilled in only three-and-one-half years.

Let us look at them.

1. A Generational Antichrist Baton

The first reason for this skepticism is because since 1967 an unidentified adult person, who will eventually sign a covenant with Israel, *must always be alive* in order to step in and quickly be revealed as the Antichrist after the rapture. If the rapture and signing of the covenant have been imminent, a potential Antichrist has been required to be somewhere, unknown to the world, during this entire time. Because it has not yet happened, some new individual must become available in each successive generation to replace the previous one who eventually gets old and dies. Therefore, a concealed Antichrist person must have been living since AD 32, 65, 70, or 1967, depending on where one thinks the rapture became imminent.

There must be what I would figuratively call a *human Antichrist baton* being passed from some person in one generation to another in each successive generation until the rapture occurs and the Antichrist is finally manifested. This requirement of a figurative Antichrist baton, while being logically necessary, is difficult to believe under the idea of the pretribulation, imminent rapture since they claim it has been imminent for so long. No person can maintain their young adulthood or live that long. By contrast, the prewrath position does not have to deal with this generational Antichrist baton problem. The reason is because there is just *a single generation in which the one and only Antichrist* needs to arise in since his future revelation is the last prophecy necessary before the rapture becomes imminent. Prewrath does not require the possibility of the Antichrist's presence to be hidden for decades, generations, or centuries as the pretribulation, present-day imminence position does. Once the world conditions are ready to accept him, then he will appear and fulfill the prophecies about him. This will be a signal to the spiritually alert followers of Christ to be prepared for great tribulation, but also to eagerly anticipate the rapture. This is exactly the teaching of Jesus to the apostles in the Olivet Discourse of Matthew 24, Mark 13, Luke 21 and by Paul in 2 Thessalonians 2.

2. The World is Not Ready … Yet!

A second logical reason for questioning "imminence since 1967" piggybacks on the first. It centers around the unlikelihood that, if the rapture were to occur, the prophesied activities brought by the Antichrist could be fulfilled in just three-and-one-half years from any time after 1967 to the present time. These details were mentioned previously (see points #1 through #3 in the list above) and would have to take place at lightning speed. Is it reasonable that, from 1967 until now, within three-and-one-half years, all nations could unify and demand each person submit to the will of one political, military, and religious leader nobody presently knows about? Is it reasonable that in just three-and-one-half years from 1967 until now this Antichrist would have been able to go into a Jewish temple (that does not presently exist), stop the sacrifices there and declare himself to be God above all other gods? This means a majority of the world's people would be willing to abandon their previous religion? Is it reasonable that there could be a successful, worldwide campaign of persecution to the point of murdering multitudes worldwide, enacted against everyone who does not follow this unknown man of lawlessness? The pretribulation teaching compels one to believe that since 1967, up until today, all these things could have been brought to completion in just 42 months after a sudden and signless rapture. All of these things will eventually happen, but it is highly improbable that they have been able to take place in such a short amount of time since 1967, given the conditions in the world today. The end result is that this pillar of pretribulation rapture's imminence teaching continues to wobble under the pressure of sound reasoning and, as we shall see, good Bible hermeneutics.

This leads to the next question:

> Do you agree it is it highly unlikely that the prophesied events of the first half of Daniel's 70th Week have been able to begin to happen at any moment since 1967 and be brought to fulfillment in just three-and-one-half years?

If this is acknowledged, there is an apparent openness to consider an alternative rapture imminence teaching. If there is hesitation to admit this, I would ask the pretribulation rapture believer to present a reasonable explanation for how the prophecies of the first half of the 70th Week could possibly start and be fulfilled in just three-and-one-half years. Try to avoid getting bogged down in a long and drawn out debate based on unreasonable speculation about what might happen to permit those events to be presently imminent. After allowing for a possible brief dialogue, make the transition into the next very important challenge with which pretribulation rapture believers are faced.

More Important Than Logical Reasoning

Not only is it illogical for the rapture to have been imminent since 1967 based on the world's conditions, it also contradicts some clear passages in the Bible.[30]

---

[30] Someone may ask, "How can you prewrath believers say these passages clearly teach what you believe when there are many good Bible teachers who interpret them a different way?" This is a very good question. My response is that a person's previous beliefs are going to influence how they evaluate something, so

Recall that pretribulationists claim that the revelation of the Antichrist cannot take place before the rapture because they think *there are no preliminary signs that need to be fulfilled beforehand.* However, Jesus taught the opposite of this when He told the disciples that some generation of His followers would go through great tribulation and see the Antichrist (Matt. 24:4-28) before He would appear and gather the elect (Matt. 24:29-31). Jesus repeatedly addresses His apostles (or some future generation of His followers) as "you" in the Olivet Discourse.[ii]

> See to it that no one misleads *you...* And *you* will be hearing of wars and rumors of war, see that *you* are not frightened... Then they will deliver *you* to tribulation and will kill *you* and *you* will be hated by all nations on account of My name... Therefore, when *you* see the abomination of desolation which was spoken of through Daniel the prophet standing in the holy place, then let those who are in Judea flee to the mountains... But pray that *your* flight may not be in in the winter or on the Sabbath for then there will be great tribulation such as has not occurred since the beginning of the world until now... Then if anyone says to *you* 'Behold, here is the Christ' or 'There He is,' do not believe him... Behold I have told *you* in advance... Now learn the parable from the fig tree, when its branch has already become tender and puts forth its leaves, *you* know that summer is near, even so *you* too when *you* see all

---

two individuals looking at the same information may come to two different conclusions. For example, the atheist believes there is no God. Therefore, he looks at the fossil record and comes to the conclusion that it is proof of evolution. Many Christians, on the other hand, believe fossils are the result of God's destruction of the world by the flood in Genesis. Each is convinced of their conclusion because it agrees with their previous assumption. Therefore, if someone has been exposed only (or primarily) to the pretribulation rapture, then he or she will look at the Bible's teaching on the end times through that lens, whether those verses actually support that position or not. It is only when presented with evidence that the pretribulation rapture conflicts with the clear teaching of the Bible that they may be willing to take off the glasses of their previous assumptions and see things differently.

> these things, recognize that He is near, right at the
> door. Truly I say to *you*, "this generation will not pass
> away until all these things take place" (Matt. 24: 4-
> 34, emphasis added).

The best interpretation of Jesus' words must be that *you* represents some generation of Christians who will face the Antichrist in the time of tribulation. The abomination of desolation they will see is another future prophecy before His return. Jesus is trying to warn them of the deception and trials they will face just before He gloriously appears in the sky to gather His chosen ones to safety in heaven before He sends His Day-of-the-Lord wrath.

> Immediately after the tribulation of those days the
> sun will be darkened, and the moon will not give its
> light, and the stars will fall from the sky, and the
> powers of the heavens will be shaken, and then the
> sign of the Son of Man will appear in the sky, and
> then all the tribes of the earth will mourn, and they
> will see the Son of Man coming on the clouds of the
> sky with power and great glory. And He will send
> forth His angels with a great trumpet, and they will
> gather together His elect from the four winds, from
> one end of the sky to the other (Matt. 24:29-31).

Simply put, Jesus is telling His disciples (or members of the future church) that *after* they have seen the abomination of desolation and experienced this tribulation, He will appear in the sky and use angels to gather His elect followers from all over the world. This is the rapture! It fits perfectly with the context of the Olivet Discourse and what Paul wrote to the Thessalonians concerning Christ's second coming for the church before the Day of the Lord:

> Now we request you, brethren, with regard to the
> coming of our Lord Jesus Christ and our gathering
> together to Him, that you may not be quickly shaken
> from your composure or be disturbed, either by a
> spirit or a message or a letter as if from us, to the
> effect that the Day of the Lord has come. Let no one
> in any way deceive you, *for it will not come unless
> the apostasy comes first, and the man of lawlessness*

is revealed, the son of destruction, who opposes and exalts himself above every so-called god or object of worship, so that he takes his seat in the temple of God, displaying himself as being God. Do you not remember that while I was still with you, I was telling you these things? And you know what restrains him now, so that in his time, he may be revealed (2 Thess. 2:1-6, emphasis added).

(See Chapter 8 for the full study on the Day of the Lord and Appendix 2 on page 153 for "the restrainer".)

Remember, the pretribulation rapture demands that a potential Antichrist must always be available, yet unrevealed, and ready to jump onto the world scene. This is necessary in order to support the belief that there are no preliminary signs before Daniel's 70th Week begins (which they mistakenly identify in its entirety as the Day of the Lord). But that is clearly contrary to Paul's statement with regard to the coming of Jesus, our gathering to Him, and the coming of the Day of the Lord. He says the apostasy and the man of sin *must come first.* These are preceding signs just as Jesus taught, and if this is the proper interpretation, it destroys the presupposition of pretribulation imminence. Which should we believe, the clear plain interpretation of the words of Jesus and the writings of the apostle Paul or an interpretation originating in the 1830's and based on questionable exegesis? The answer is clear: Jesus and Paul agree that there are prophesied signs before the rapture will happen. The final one that makes the rapture imminent is the abomination of desolation, the appearance of Antichrist in the Jewish holy place at the midpoint of the 70th Week. This will all take place *before the Day of the Lord*. It cannot be any more obvious than this. (see Appendix 3 on page 159)

Summary of the Pretribulation Imminence Problems

In addition to the prophecies that must be fulfilled before the rapture can occur, the pretribulation system must deal with three other obstacles to an "any moment" rapture. The first is the requirement of an ongoing presence of a hidden Antichrist on earth. The second is the improbability of the events of the first three-and-one-half years after the rapture being able to happen in light of the current state of affairs in the world. Third, and perhaps most significantly, it has to overcome the contradiction with their interpretation and the clear words of Christ in the Olivet Discourse and Paul's letter to the Thessalonians. Both indicate that Christians will be in the presence of the Antichrist and the great tribulation *before* Jesus appears, raptures them, and the Day of the Lord's wrath immediately follows.

However, the prewrath scenario does not have these problems. The following diagram shows why since *the beginning of rapture imminence is the Abomination of Desolation* at the midpoint of Daniel's 70th Week. The Antichrist's rise to power results in the great tribulation, but the long-awaited rapture brings that period to an end and allows for the beginning of God's wrath.

Correct Imminence Timeline

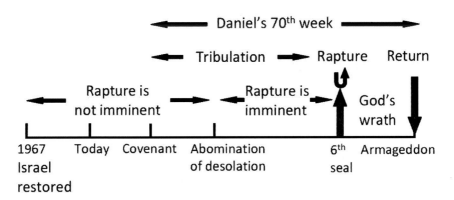

The Toughest Question for the Pretribulationist

The next point of our inquiry as we near the end of this part of the trial deals with the most recent and probably the most problematic passage for the pretribulation rapture believer to explain in this examination:

> Can you agree that the most reasonable interpretation
> of Jesus' teaching in the Olivet Discourse and Paul's
> message in 2 Thessalonians 2:1-6 is that the
> Antichrist must be present before the appearing of

> Jesus, the rapture, and the arrival of the Day of the
> Lord?

One of the leading pretribulation rapture scholars I talked to admitted that this passage is the most difficult one for him to explain in light of his belief in an "any moment" rapture. Therefore, this question must be taken seriously and not glossed over. If someone admits that the best interpretation of the words of Jesus and Paul is that Antichrist will be revealed before the rapture, then the belief that the rapture could presently happen at any moment without any signs is false and some other interpretation must be adopted.

A Question of Assessment, but Not the End of the Trial

A question at this point of the trial evaluates the effect of this challenge against the pretribulation pillar that the rapture has been imminent over the many centuries of church history.

> As a result of these questions, has this process of
> reasoning raised doubts in your mind that the rapture
> could presently happen at any moment?

If it has, then I wholeheartedly encourage continuing the conversation (or reading the rest of this book). What remains will contain more important follow-up information in the trial, although it will not consist of a lot of questions. In keeping with the trial metaphor, the rest could be compared to the closing arguments. They will reveal more genuine difficulties with the pretribulation rapture teaching, but also the presentation of solutions to these problems based on the prewrath interpretation.

ⁱ **Response to the Argument: 'God Can Do Anything!'**

One of my pretribulation rapture teaching friends responded to my reasoning that if the rapture were to happen today, there is not enough time in just three-and-one-half years from right now for the events of the first half of the tribulation to be fulfilled. He said, "These prophesied events are possible in such a short amount of time because *God can do anything!*"

Of course, I agree that God can do anything, according to His perfect character and will. God is able to supernaturally intervene in the world's events such that they may happen in a way that people may not normally expect. Nobody expected the walls of Jericho to suddenly collapse when the people shouted, but they did. Nobody expected Paul to get suddenly converted while he was persecuting the Christians, but he did. We could go on and on. Yet, these were exceptions and not the rule. The rest of the cities in the Promised Land were not defeated in the same way Jericho was, nor did all the scribes and Pharisees have conversion experiences like Paul's. It must be acknowledged that God usually works out His prophetic plan for the world over the normal course of time throughout history. I also do not disagree with my pretrib friends that things are moving quickly toward the end-time events described in the Bible. More than once, I have responded: "Yes, we are getting closer each day, each year, each decade, and each generation. However, today we are still not yet to the place where those clearly defined events of the first half of Daniel's 70th Week could all be fulfilled in just three-and-one-half years."

Am I saying it is impossible for the Second Coming to happen in our generation? No, but I am contending that the generation of alert Christians *must first* see *the signs* that Jesus told the disciples would happen before His coming and the end of the age. Our generation has not seen them yet. If we do, then we would be that generation.

The most fundamental and obvious truth of the prewrath view, which is supported by the Scriptures and common sense, is that one generation of the church will recognize the Antichrist and the events that come along with his actions before Jesus will return to remove His church. The Lord spoke of these events in the Olivet Discourse in Matthew 24 and Mark 13, but most specifically in Luke 21:28: "Now when these things begin to take place, straighten up and lift your heads because your redemption is drawing near."

In this passage, Jesus is telling that generation of His followers that when these things take place, *then* His coming to rapture them out of the tribulation will be imminent, and it will cut short the affliction they are experiencing. Until then, the significant players and conditions are not in place to reasonably allow the events immediately before and after the rapture to unfold. The rapture is not presently imminent because the gospel has not been preached to the entire world, the Antichrist and the false prophet have not been revealed, and many parts of the world are not yet ready to surrender to a one-world dictator. However, at some point in the future, the Great Commission will be near completion and the nations will be willing to give up their individual sovereignty and accept an Antichrist character to save the world when he comes on the scene. This will then be soon followed by Jesus' appearance at some unknown time. He will rescue the persecuted living Christians, raise the dead ones at the rapture, and send His punishment upon the unbelievers.

ii Who Are the 'You' in the Olivet Discourse?

Pretribulationists tell us that when Jesus uses the pronoun "you" in the Olivet Discourse (Matt. 24-25, Luke 21, and Mark 13), He is referring only to Jewish people, the nation of Israel, during the tribulation. They argue that the "you" cannot be talking about Christians since they claim the church must have already been raptured before the tribulation. Three reasons they often give us to support their understanding are as follows:

1) Matthew's gospel was written to the Jews, so Jesus was addressing the apostles as Jews and not as Christians.

2) The church had not been established at the time of the Olivet Discourse, so Jesus was talking to them as members of the nation of Israel, not as Christians.

3) Since the Olivet Discourse concerns the time of Daniel's 70th Week, which only relates to the Jews and their capital city of Jerusalem, it does not apply to the dispensation of followers of Jesus who are members of the church.

Here are some problems with this line of reasoning:

1) There are no verses in Matthew indicating it was written only to the Jewish people. That is an unfounded assumption.

2) Mark 13 and Luke 21 also contain the Olivet Discourse, and Jesus uses the same pronoun, "you," to answer the same questions. Those other two gospels are not said to be written to the Jews. In fact, Luke's gospel is specifically written by a Gentile to a Gentile (Luke 1:1-3).

3) Ironically, the only time the Greek word for "church" (*ekklēsia*) is used in any of the gospels is in Matthew 16:18 and 18:17. One must wonder why a supposedly "Jewish gospel" would be the only one out of the four that uses the word "church."

4) The people Jesus is addressing in the Olivet Discourse were His true believing followers who would soon become the leaders of His community of Jewish and Gentile followers in the church. He was not speaking to the apostles as simply members of the nation of Israel. The first-century church was primarily made up of Jews and a few Gentiles (over the centuries, the proportions have obviously changed). However, no matter which gospel you read, the most clear and simple interpretation is that this message is to the multi-ethnic church.

5) Pretribulationists say the first part of the discourse, Matthew 24:3-31, does not apply to the church, but rather only to Israel during the tribulation. Then they turn around and claim that the rest of His discourse from Matthew 24:32 – 25:46 has

application to all who are in the church, especially Matthew 24:36-37: "No one knows the day or the hour of His coming." How can they use this as a proof of imminence for the rapture of the church, but take it from a context that they say is intended only for Israel? We must answer, "They can't!"

Just as people often try to fit the proverbial "square peg into a round hole," pretribulation scholars are attempting to force the text of Matthew 24 to apply only to Israel and not to the New Testament church. They must do this in order to keep the church separated from the Antichrist and out of the tribulation.

CHAPTER 7

IMMINENCE AND CURRENT WORLD EVENTS

Despite the fact that pretribulation rapture teachers disagree with the prewrath timing of events, it is noteworthy that many leading pretribulation rapture teachers do agree, to some extent, with the prewrath assessment of current events? This is interesting considering that, by doing so, they are undermining their own position that the rapture has been and presently is still imminent. For example, John Walvoord writes (emphasis added):

> But if there are no signs for the rapture itself, what are the legitimate grounds for believing that the rapture could be *especially near this generation*? The answer is not found in any prophetic events predicted *before* the rapture but in understanding the events that *will follow* the rapture. Just as history was prepared for Christ's first coming, in a similar way *history is preparing* for the events leading up to His Second Coming . . . If this is the case, it leads to the inevitable conclusion that *the rapture may be excitingly near.*[31]

---

[31] John F. Walvoord, *Armageddon, Oil and the Middle East Crisis* (Grand Rapids: Zondervan, 1991 revised), 217.

Except for his statement that there are *no prophetic events predicted before the rapture*, anyone who holds the prewrath position could agree with everything else that he said. Dr. Walvoord admits that there are prophetic events that will *follow the rapture*, allowing us to presently know the Second Coming is near. His statement "it leads to the inevitable conclusion" indicates he is using logical reasoning in making these statements. This is a clear inconsistency in the pretribulation view of imminence. How can they claim that the rapture is imminent today, without any signs, and then say we are getting "excitedly near" to the rapture because history is preparing for events leading up to the Second Coming? If the rapture is truly imminent, without any preliminary indicators, there should no observable current events leading to our being stimulated with excitement about it. Nor would there be anything we can now observe to indicate that we are nearer to the rapture today than we were yesterday or at any time in the past. At best, the only thing they can logically say is that we are one day closer as each day passes, not by seeing events that align with biblical prophecy. Any statement that we are "especially near" to the rapture contradicts their foundational pillar of any moment rapture without any signs before it.

Another leading pretribulation rapture teacher, Thomas Ice, makes a statement similarly contradictory to his own position. In his article "How Signs of the Times Relate to the Rapture and the Second Coming," published in the *Pre-Trib Perspectives Journal*, Dr. Ice identifies three possible views that pretribulation teachers hold concerning *how current events relate to the imminent rapture*. Here is my summary of his discussion, followed by my response:

1) "Loose view." Those holding this view see certain current events today *fulfilling biblical prophecies for Israel*. In his article, Dr. Ice disagrees with this position primarily because it breaks down the dispensational distinction between the church and Israel. From a pretribulational perspective, I see a more obvious problem with this view because the pretribulation rapture position holds that no prophecies need to be fulfilled before the rapture will occur. Thus, if there are prophecies "presently being fulfilled," this directly contradicts their own teaching on imminence. In spite of this contradiction, other pretribulationists do not seem to ever confront them with this inconsistency. While teachers of the pretribulation rapture do not have to agree on every detail of their position, they should not disagree on the most foundational pillar of their teaching on imminence.[i]

2) "Strict view." This is defined as there being *no observable signs that must take place before the rapture*. Thus, these pretribulation teachers do not pay attention to global happenings. In their minds, current events have *nothing* to do with the any moment appearing of Jesus to rapture the church. Of these three pretribulation perspectives, this one is the most logically consistent with their teaching on imminence.

3) "Moderate view." This is the position held by Dr. Ice as the best of the three. This position contends that none of the current happenings are prerequisite for the rapture to take place. However, there are some present events that are *setting the stage for what will eventually take place in the tribulation*. In this article, he writes: "The positioning of players and events related to God's plan for the world, after the rapture, during the future tribulation is increasingly casting shadows upon the current church age. This results in an *intensifying anticipation of the any moment rapture* which must take place before events of the tribulation can unfold" (emphasis added). In these comments, Dr. Ice is basically repeating Dr. Walvoord's earlier statement. Notice his continued interpretation of an "any moment" rapture before the tribulation. Then he turns around and makes a direct correlation between the current positioning of players and events with what will take place during that time. This leads to the question: Why would there be any *shadow upon the current church age* from the prophesied tribulation if there supposedly are no signs that need to occur before the rapture? Second, if there are *no necessary pre-rapture events to observe*, there should be no increasing expectation based on present events.

In Dr. Walvoord's and Dr. Ice's conclusions, they both say that because we are observing certain events, we should have "excitement" and "intensifying anticipation" as we recognize the rapture is quickly approaching. They clearly imply that the events we see happening in the world are making the rapture *more imminent* as time passes. Thus, instead of labeling Dr. Ice's preferred view as "the moderate view," we might better name it the *partial imminence* view. Just as one cannot logically say that a woman is partially pregnant, one cannot logically think that a signless rapture is *more imminent* based on seeing certain events occur.[32] Either a woman is pregnant or she is not. It does not matter how close she is to having the baby. She does not become "more pregnant" because everyone can see her stomach growing in size. Likewise, an "any moment," imminent rapture does not become "more imminent" as we see contemporary events unfold. These statements about the rapture becoming more imminent need to be challenged if pretribulationists truly believe in their definition of imminence.

I would, however, agree that, based on the unfolding of current events, the rapture is closer than ever before. Prewrath believers point to the statements of Jesus and Paul, who gave us signs to observe which must take place before Christ comes back for the church and prior to the outpouring of God's wrath. Remember in the last chapter how careful scrutinized thinking was used, along with clear scriptural teaching, to show the rapture cannot happen at any moment right now.

The prewrath interpretation is the most logically consistent with the constant unfolding events in the world and also with the plain reading of all the Bible passages related to Christ's second coming. His return can reasonably be expected only *after* the yet-to-be fulfilled prophecies about the Antichrist and the tribulation have come to pass. Jesus even emphasized this fact when he said, "Behold, I have told you in advance… When you see all these things, recognize that He is near, right at the door" (Matt. 24: 25, 33). The context favors the "all these things" being the manifestation of the Antichrist and the persecution that will be experienced by anyone who does not submit to him. We are now witnessing the stage being set for those end-time events but the rapture cannot

---

[32] Credit for this observation goes to prewrath teacher Justus Stull, who made this observation in personal conversation about this position held by many pretribulation rapture teachers.

happen at any moment now.

The following three passages will be understood by some generation of alert Christians who will recognize the presence of the Antichrist and conclude that *the rapture has become imminent*. First is Matthew 24:3-31, where Jesus gave warnings and signs for His followers to look for in answering their question about His second coming. Second is 2 Thessalonians 2:1-5, where Paul mentioned two events, the apostasy and the revealing of the man of sin, that must precede the Day of the Lord. Third is Revelation 6:1-17, where God reveals to John that all the seven seals must be removed from the scroll before God's wrath will come upon His enemies. There is no discrepancy with the prewrath understanding of the rapture *becoming imminent* in the future and the conditions of the world before and after the rapture takes place.

What Are Christians Supposed to Be Looking For?

The thought that Christians will find themselves in the presence of the Antichrist and the tribulation may sound like heresy to those who hold strongly to the teaching of the rapture being imminent right now. They will often repeat the mantra: "We are looking for Christ, not the Antichrist," which is based on the following passage from Titus:

> For the grace of God has appeared, bringing salvation to all men, instructing us to deny ungodliness and worldly desires and to live sensibly, righteously and godly in the present age, looking for the blessed hope and the appearing of the glory of our great God and Savior, Christ Jesus. (Titus 2:13)

I already mentioned this verse in the list of proof texts in Chapter 2 that pretribulation rapture teachers use to support their view of rapture imminence. Based on this verse, they say Christians should be looking for the arrival of Christ, not the Antichrist. In other words, we are expecting Jesus to come and rapture us to heaven before the Antichrist and the tribulation arrive on the world scene. On the surface, that is a catchy phrase, but the interpretation has some difficulties. I briefly responded in that section of this book that

Titus 2:13 does not clearly teach imminence because to look forward
to something does not clearly mean it can happen at any moment.
There are three additional details in this passage that weaken its
support for an any moment rapture.

First, the common lexical meanings of the Greek word
prosdechomai are "to expect," "wait for," or possibly "look for"
something.[33] There are other nuances as well, since the *New
American Standard Bible* has the following for the Greek word in
the fourteen times it is found in the New Testament: 1) "wait for"
(five times); 2) "look for" (three times); 3) "receive" (three times);
4) "accept" (two times); and 5) "cherish" (once). None of these uses
of the word here come close to meaning "something that is the next
event to happen." The claim of an "any moment" imminent rapture
in Titus 2:13 is being forced into that verse.

Second, pretribulation teachers say "the blessed hope" is the "any
moment" rapture, but is different from the "the appearing of the
glory of our God and Savior Jesus Christ." They teach these two
actions are separated by the seven years of Daniel's 70th Week. The
rapture will happen suddenly, without any display of glory, before
the tribulation. They say "the appearance of the glory" event will be
Christ's spectacular second coming in great power later, at the end
of the tribulation, when Jesus returns to the earth. Contrasted with
this is the prewrath understanding that the "blessed hope" and "the
glorious appearance" are the same event, a single coming. His
second coming will bring two things at once. First, it will provide
the promised and assured deliverance of Christians from the
Antichrist's persecution as it cuts short the tribulation (Matt. 24:22).
Second, it will immediately begin God's wrath upon the Antichrist
and his associates (Joel 2:31; Matt. 24:29-30; Rev. 6:12-17). The
unity of this single glorious appearance to rapture the righteous and
punish the ungodly is unmistakably stated by Paul:

> For after all it is only just for God to *repay with
> affliction those who afflict you, and to give relief to*

---

[33] *A Greek-English Lexicon of the New Testament,* by Baur, Arndt, and Gingrich
(Chicago: University of Chicago Press, Fourth Revised and Augmented Edition,
1957), def. 2, 719.

you who are afflicted and to us as well when the Lord Jesus will be revealed from heaven with His mighty angels in flaming fire, dealing out retribution to those who do not know God and to those who do not obey the gospel of our Lord Jesus. These will pay the penalty of eternal destruction, away from the presence of the Lord and from the glory of His power, when He comes to be glorified in His saints on that day, and to be marveled at among all who have believed. (2 Thess. 1:6-10, emphasis added)

This revelation of Christ from heaven is best interpreted to be *a single event*, rather than two separate actions separated by seven years. The relief of the saints and the beginning of the retribution on Christ's enemies will happen at the same time.

Third, contextually the pretribulation interpretation does not make sense to motivate the Thessalonians to godly living if the "blessed hope" and "glorious appearing" are different, split apart by seven years. Why would Paul tell his Christian readers in Titus 2:11-12 to be motivated to live holy lives by a glorious second coming of Jesus at the end of the seven-year tribulation if they will already have been taken away to heaven by a pretribulation blessed hope rapture? It only makes sense that they would be motivated to live righteously in the midst of the tribulation if Christ's "revelation from heaven" is both the blessed hope/rapture and His glorious appearing/second coming just before God's wrath arrives.

Titus 2:11-13 encourages Christians to be alert and wait for the glorious appearing of Jesus at some unknown time when He will rapture the surviving believers out of the persecution of the Antichrist's tribulation to be with Him. But to state that "the blessed hope" is the next prophecy to be fulfilled and can happen at any moment before the tribulation is unfounded.

So, the answer to the question "What are Christians supposed to be looking for?" is clearly taught by both Jesus and Paul without any straining of the text. The church is warned to first look for deceptions during the Antichrist's presence and the tribulation he will bring. This will be a signal to Christ's disciples that their deliverance by rapture is soon to follow

.

---

[i] A Pretribulation Rapture Conference about Bible Prophecies Being Fulfilled Now

I recently received an advertisement for a pretribulation rapture prophecy conference. It is an example of the "loose view" of the timing of the rapture because they claim "current events are said to be fulfilling Bible prophecies" in spite of their own teaching that the rapture is the next prophecy to be fulfilled. Here is the text of the promotion I received:

A One-of-a-Kind Prophecy Conference

> The 2nd Annual Blessed Hope Prophecy Forum is coming back… The three-day event begins on October 12-14th, 2018. 33 well-known speakers and Bible teachers will be joining us, many of them names we all recognize like … [names omitted) … and many more gifted men and women. Our speakers come from all walks of life. Pastors, professors, scientists, archaeologists, politicians, military experts, authors, and long-time radio and TV personalities. They'll be discussing many diverse subjects that you will likely never hear in church! *Current world events are fulfilling Bible prophecy at a rapid pace."*

Remember that pretribulationists believe the next prophecy to be fulfilled is the rapture. Then, at the same time, they are telling us that many global happenings are biblical prophecies that are being fulfilled. I took the initiative to communicate with the people promoting this conference and ask about this inconsistency. They sent the following response: (emphasis added)

> Thanks for the feedback. The speakers at this conference that we are helping promote would mostly all fall into the category of pretrib, and it would be safe to say, in agreement with you, that this view requires no prophecy to be fulfilled for the rapture to take place. However, and I believe this to be the view of the speakers of this conference, *there are other events that are predicted to happen that do have prerequisites, separate and different to the rapture.* I hope this clears it up.

No, that does not clear it up. In fact, the more you dig, the more contradictions surface. If the pretribulation rapture is true and there are no prophecies left to be fulfilled before it will occur, then there cannot be current world events fulfilling biblical prophecies before the rapture. It is clear this individual thinks that there is no problem in having exceptions to this teaching. If so, he is ignoring the fact that any Bible prophecy is a prophecy, whether it deals with an end-time event or not. An example of this is Jesus' prophecy about Peter's death in John 20:18-20, which I discussed in Chapter 3. Jesus did not make this prediction to Peter in the context of teaching about eschatology. It was a personal prophecy about Peter's life. However, that prophecy impacts eschatology because, at the time it was given, it was a prophecy that would have to take place before an imminent rapture could happen. The *personal* prophecy about Peter must happen first, before the *eschatological* prophecy of the rapture could occur. The personal prophecies about Paul and the prediction of the destruction of the temple are two other examples dealt with earlier in this book. One must assume that the person who wrote the above response would classify these prophecies as other prophesied events that are "separate and different to the rapture." However, this is not good logic nor Bible hermeneutics. When he tells me that he is in agreement that the pretribulation rapture requires no prophecy to be fulfilled before the rapture takes place, that must be understood to mean exactly what it says: *There is no Bible prophecy required—period.* According to what their own position teaches, there can be no prophecies that can take place during the church age before the rapture, even ones that are not directly related to eschatology.

It is apparent that the conclusions that these present-day prophetic fulfillments mentioned by the pretribulation prophecy conference speakers create a contradiction with their own teaching about imminence but they do not realize it. Of course, exceptions exist if a prophecy is about something that we know will happen after the rapture, such as the Great White Throne Judgment or the casting of the Antichrist and the false prophet into the lake of fire. If those teachers who hold to the pretribulation rapture position believe there are exceptions to their clear statement about no prophecy being necessary before an "any moment" rapture, then they need to indicate that in their definition about imminence. I have not been able to find a single pretribulation rapture statement that contains an explanation of exceptions to their expression about imminence. In the meantime, many of these teachers continue to proclaim that Bible prophecies are currently being fulfilled in world events, so we are getting nearer to the rapture, yet the rapture is supposed to be the next Bible prophecy to be fulfilled. *This is a serious contradiction to their entire belief system.* Also, those pretribulationists who do not agree with this "loose view" (as defined by Dr. Ice, see Chapter 7) have an obligation to confront their brethren who are writing and speaking about it, since it weakens the credibility of their teaching on imminence.

CHAPTER 8

THE DAY OF THE LORD, WHAT AND WHEN IS IT?

The results of a trial can be completely changed when it is discovered that there has been a mistaken identity of the accused person. Likewise, this trial is going to be dramatically impacted when a critical concept is correctly defined. This biblical term that will be closely examined in this chapter is "the Day of the Lord." One pretribulation rapture scholar commented on the significance of this expression:

> Pre- and posttribulationists agree that the Day of the Lord bears directly on the time of the rapture… Premillennialists do not debate when the Day of the Lord will end, only when it will begin. — Charles Ryrie[34]

Dr. Ryrie's book, *What You Should Know About the Rapture*, was published in 1981. At that time, the big debate was between the pretribulation and posttribulation positions. Mid-tribulation was still a minor position, and prewrath had not yet been developed, so neither of those was included in his discussion. However, the point is simply to see that improper identification of the Day of the Lord,

---

[34] Charles Ryrie, *What You Should Know About the Rapture*, 94.

and when it begins, results in a faulty recognition of when Christians will escape God's wrath by the rapture.

Christians Will Escape God's Wrath, Not Satan's Wrath

One thing that all four major rapture positions agree on is that the church will not go through God's eschatological wrath on earth. This promise is recorded by the apostle Paul:

> For they themselves report about us what kind of a reception we had with you, and how you turned to God from idols to serve a living and true God, and to wait for His Son from heaven, whom He raised from the dead, that is Jesus, *who rescues us from the wrath to come…For God has not destined us for wrath*, but for obtaining salvation through our Lord Jesus Christ. (1 Thess. 1:9-10 and 5:9, emphasis added)

Those are two great and exciting promises for every Christian. It must be remembered, though, that there are other promises that are not so pleasant. Among them is that some Christians will experience persecution and tribulation, even unto death. There are many places in the world, especially America, where freedom of religion is protected by the government. However, in many other places, following Christ is far more dangerous as the Bible informs us:

> Remember the word that I said to you, "A slave is not greater than his master." If they persecuted Me, they will also persecute you …In the world you will have tribulation … All who desire to live godly in Christ Jesus will be persecuted. (John 15:20; 16:33; 2 Tim. 3:12)

The purpose of this chapter is to show that there is a difference between the future persecution of God's people at the hand of the Antichrist during the tribulation and the judgments upon unbelievers as a result of the Day-of-the-Lord wrath. To confuse the two, equating them, prevents one from properly understanding the starting point for the Day of the Lord. This, in turn, distorts one's ability to know when the rapture will take place.

Those who say the rapture can presently happen at any moment understand the Day of the Lord *to be the same as all* of Daniel's 70th Week and that it will last the entire seven years. This perspective is defended by the following three teachers:

> It [the Day of the Lord] includes the tribulation time. — Dr. John F. Walvoord[35]

> The Day of the Lord includes the whole program from the beginning of the tribulation period. — Dr. Dwight Pentecost[36]

> According to the chronology Jesus presents in the Olivet Discourse, the day of the Lord will precede His return. This period of time, also known as the tribulation, will be seven years long. — Glen Kreider[37] (Note: by "return," Kreider means Christ's Second Coming in glory at the *end* of the tribulation.[i])

It is also important to know that teachers of the pretribulation rapture say that all of the events during these seven years are caused by God, coming directly from His hand. Prewrath disagrees, making a distinction between the wrath of the Antichrist against Christians during the tribulation of Daniel's 70th Week—depicted by the breaking of each of the first five seals —and the wrath of God, which arrives after the opening of the scroll. In fact, it is with the breaking of the sixth seal that we see the appearance of Jesus at the rapture and the announcement that the wrath of God is about to come. God's wrath takes place during the remainder of Daniel's 70th Week and is administered by God's angels. This wrath is represented by the contents of the scroll after the 7th and final seal is removed. These are the trumpets and the bowls judgments.

---

[35] Dr. John F. Walvoord, *The Thessalonian Epistles* (Dunham Publishing, 1955), 117.

[36] Dr. Dwight Pentecost, *Things to Come,* 552.

[37] Glen Kreider, *The Rapture and the Day of the Lord,* article in book *Evidence for the Rapture: A Biblical Case for Pretribulationism*, edited by John Hart), 82.

The following two charts will show how the pretribulation and prewrath systems understand the periods of tribulation and wrath during Daniel's 70th Week.

Pretribulation Daniel's 70th Week

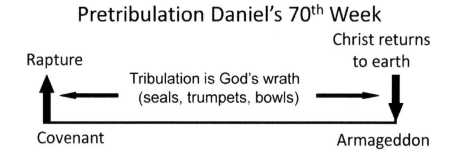

Prewrath Daniel's 70th Week

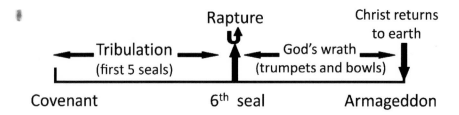

If pretribulationism is correct in saying that the tribulation is the same as the Day of the Lord's wrath and it lasts the entire 70th Week/seven years, there should be no exegetical confusion with the other related Bible passages. Likewise, if the prewrath teaching that the tribulation is distinct from the Day of the Lord during the seven years, then it, too, must not contradict the same passages. It is admittedly easy to understand at first glance why pretribulationists recognize the tribulation as being the same as God's wrath. Both the tribulation and the Day of the Lord will occur near the end of the age in Daniel's 70th Week. They both depict terrible times, unmatched in all of human history. However, one cannot stop with just these two similarities and conclude that they are the same. We have to look at the contexts of all of the "Day of the Lord" passages and determine whether there are any differences between what is described by them and what is said to happen in the passages about the tribulation.

The Old Testament and "the Day of the Lord"

The following study is critical in the debate about the timing of the rapture. It is a list of the Old Testament passages that contain the term "the Day of the Lord." Before we look at this list, it would be good to go over one of the lesser-known rules of hermeneutics because it influences the proper understanding of this term. This rule is called the Law of First Mention, also called the Rule of First Occurrence:

> The Law of First Mention may be said to be the principle that requires one to go to that portion of the Scriptures where a doctrine is mentioned for the first time and to study the first occurrence of the same in order to get the fundamental inherent meaning of that doctrine.[38]

Certain aspects of these verses have been emphasized to draw attention to details that are considered significant. This is not a detailed exegesis, but simply a survey of the texts in order to provide a general understanding of how the Day of the Lord should be understood. (emphasis added)

Obadiah

Obadiah 15: "For the day of the Lord draws near *on all the nations.*"

Joel

Joel 1:15: "Alas for the day. For the day of the Lord is near, and it

---

[38] Dr. David L. Cooper, *Hermeneutics: The Science of Interpreting the Scriptures,* The Biblical Research Society, www.messianicassociation.org/ezine21-dc.hermeneutics-messianic.htm.

will come as *destruction from the Almighty.*"

Joel 2:1-2: "Let all the inhabitants of the land tremble, for the day of the Lord is coming, surely it is near. A day of darkness and gloom, a day of clouds and thick darkness…*there has never been anything like it nor will there be again after it.*"

Joel 2:10-11: "Before them the earth quakes, the heavens tremble, *the sun and the moon grow dark and the stars lose their brightness.* And the Lord utters His voice before His army, surely His camp is very great, for strong is He who carries out His word. The day of the Lord is indeed great and very awesome, and who can endure it?"

Joel 2:30-31: "And I will display wonders in the sky and on the earth, blood, fire, and columns of smoke. *The sun will be turned into darkness, and the moon into blood, before* the great day and awesome day of the Lord comes.*"* (Note: Notice the word "before.")

Joel 3:14-16: "Multitudes, multitudes in the valley of decision, for the day of the Lord is near in the valley of decision. *The sun and moon grow dark and the stars lose their brightness* and the Lord roars from Zion and utters His voice from Jerusalem, and the heavens and earth tremble, but *the Lord is a refuge for His people and a stronghold to the sons of Israel.*"

Amos

Amos 5:18-20: "Woe to you who long for the day of the Lord. Why would you long for the day of the Lord? That day will be darkness, not light. It will be as though a man fled from a lion only to meet a bear, as though he entered his house and rested his hand on the wall only to have a snake bite him. Will not the day of' the Lord be darkness not light, pitch dark without a ray of brightness?" (NIV)

Isaiah

Isaiah 2:12-21: "For the day of the Lord of hosts shall be upon everyone who is *proud and lofty*, and upon everyone who is *lifted up*, and he shall be brought low, … and the loftiness of man shall be bowed down, and the haughtiness of men shall be made low, *and the Lord alone shall be exalted in that day.* And the idols he shall utterly abolish. And they shall go into holes of the rocks, and into the caves of the earth, for fear of the Lord and for the glory of his majesty, when he ariseth to shake terribly the earth. In that day a man shall cast his idols of silver, and his idols of gold, which they made each one for himself to worship, to the moles and to the bats; to go into the clefts of the rocks, and into the tops of the ragged rocks, for fear of the Lord and the glory of his majesty, when he ariseth to shake terribly the earth." (KJV) (Note: "the Lord is the only person exalted during that day.")

Isaiah 13:6-11: "Wail, for the day of the Lord is near, it will come as *destruction from the Almighty.* Therefore, all hands will fall limp, and every man's heart shall melt, and they shall be terrified. Pains and anguish will take hold of them, they will writhe like a woman in labor, they will look at one another in astonishment, their faces aflame. Behold the day of the Lord is coming, cruel, with fury and burning anger, to make the land a desolation, and He will *exterminate its sinners* from it. For *the stars of heaven and their constellations will not flash forth their light, the sun will be dark when it rises and the moon will not shed its light.* Then I will *punish the world for its evil, and the wicked for their iniquity*, I will also put an end to *the arrogance of the proud.*"

Ezekiel

Ezekiel 13:3-5: "Thus says the Lord God 'Woe to the foolish prophets who are following their own spirit and have seen nothing. O Israel, your prophets have been like foxes among ruins. You have not gone up into the breaches, nor did you build the wall around the house of Israel to stand in the battle on the day of the Lord.'"

Ezekiel 30:2-3: "Wail, alas for the day, for the day is near, even the day of the Lord is near. It will be a day of clouds, a time of *doom for the nations.*"

Zephaniah

Zephaniah 1:7- 2:3: "Be silent before the Lord God. For the day of the Lord is near, for the Lord has prepared a sacrifice, He has consecrated His guests. Then it will come about on the day of the Lord's sacrifice that I will punish the princes, the king's sons, and all who clothe themselves with foreign garments… Near is the great day of the Lord, near and coming very quickly. Listen, the day of the Lord! In it the warrior cries out bitterly. The day of wrath is that day, a day of trouble and distress, a day of destruction and desolation, a day of darkness and gloom, a day of clouds and thick darkness… and I will bring distress on men, so they will walk like the blind because they have sinned against the Lord, and their blood will be poured out like dust and their flesh like dung. Neither their silver nor their gold will be able to deliver them on the day of the Lord's wrath, and *all the earth will be devoured in the fire of His jealousy for He will make a complete end, indeed a terrifying one of all the inhabitants of the earth*… Gather yourselves together, yes gather ... before the burning anger of the Lord comes upon you, before the day of the Lord's anger comes upon you. *Seek the Lord, all you humble* of the earth who have carried out His ordinances, seek righteousness, seek humility. *Perhaps you will be hidden* in the day of the Lord's anger. (Note: It appears some will escape God's wrath.)

Malachi

Malachi 4:1,5: Behold, the day is coming, burning like a furnace, and all the arrogant and every evildoer will be like chaff; and the day that is coming will set them ablaze… Behold, I am going to *send you Elijah the prophet before* the coming of the great and terrible day of the Lord.

If we apply the Rule of First Mention to the Day of the Lord, the foundation of our overall understanding will be formed based on what these Old Testament passages reveal about it. So, we must ask, what themes are found throughout these passages? Biblical scholarship has established that there were some days of the Lord (note small "d") that occurred in past Old Testament history. These were times when God would carry out His wrath for the sins of certain people groups, including unbelieving Jews. These could be considered "local" and "historical" days of the Lord as opposed to the future eschatological Day of the Lord. Prewrath teacher Dr. Alan Kurschner explains the distinction between the two (emphasis mine):

> My purpose is to describe a biblical picture of eschatological judgment; however, we need to be aware that the biblical prophets could also speak of a historical day of the Lord's judgment in their own times (e.g. Joel 1:15; 2:1,11; Amos 5:18; Ezekiel 13:5; Lamentations 1:12; 2:1). The most noted historical day of the Lord judgments were the downfall of the Northern kingdom in 722 B.C., the end of Nineveh in 612 B.C., the fall of Jerusalem and Judah of the Southern kingdom in 586 B.C. The prophets often used these judgments as a pattern or *foreshadowing for the larger-in-scope eschatological judgment.* [39]

This eschatological Day of the Lord has also been referred to by Bible teacher Charles Cooper as "the Granddaddy of them all" in light of its uniqueness and much greater magnitude. How does one distinguish between the past historical days of the Lord and the eschatological Day of the Lord? Discernment is made by determining whether the events described in those passages were smaller more localized ones that were completely fulfilled at some time in past history or whether they are portraying judgment that is universal in scope and for which we are still waiting.

The first list will consist of characteristics of the eschatological and grand Day of the Lord that are derived directly from these Old Testament passages. It is very important that, taking everything into account, nothing is added or subtracted from the understanding of this concept from God's Word. We must avoid distorting *the original meaning* intended by God.

---

[39] Dr. Alan Kurschner, *Antichrist Before the Day of the Lord* (Pompton Lakes, NJ: Eschatos Publishing, 2013), 112.

1. It will be unique in the history of the world (Joel 2:2,10-11).

2. It will result in total global destruction (Ob. 15; Joel 2:1, 3:15; Ezek. 30:3; Zeph. 1:18).

3. It comes directly and only from God (Joel 1:15, 2:1,11; Isa. 13:6).

4. There is universal darkening of the sun, moon and stars (aka. cosmic disturbances; Joel 2:10, 30-31, 3:14-15; Isa. 13:10).

5. Only God will be exalted during that time (Isa. 2:11).

6. It will be sometime soon in the future (Obadiah 15; Joel 1:15, 2:1; Isa. 13:6; Ezek. 30:3; Zeph. 1:7).

7. It is God's angry punishment/wrath (Amos 5:18-20; Isa. 13:11; Zeph. 1:8-2:3).

8. It is directed only against the sinful and prideful living people (Isa. 2:12-17, 13:11; Eze. 13:3-5; Zeph. 1:8-18; Mal. 4:1).

9. The wicked will be terrified and try to escape (Isa. 2:19-21).

10. Some humble people will be hidden and protected during it (Joel 3:16, Zeph. 2:3).

11. There will be signs before it arrives (Joel 2:30-31; Mal. 4:5).

Next, we will consider some of the things that pretribulation rapture teachers say will take place during the Day of the Lord, *according to how they define it*. Remember their claim is that all seven years of Daniel's 70th Week is God's wrath. If this is true, they are contending that the following characteristics and events are part of the Day of the Lord:

1. It will begin when Israel makes a covenant with a political leader in the attempt to bring them peace.

2. There will be wars and rumors of wars as nations rise up against nations.

3. There will be worldwide spiritual deception through the influence of many antichrists.

4. There will be one particular leading Antichrist, who is helped by a miracle-working assistant referred to as the false prophet.

5. Together, they will attempt to persuade the entire human race to submit to the Antichrist's political, economic, and religious demands.

6. The climax is when the Antichrist enters a Jewish holy place and demands to be worshipped as God.

7. During this time, those refusing to submit will be persecuted and possibly martyred.

8. There will be multitudes who come to faith in Jesus Christ.

9. There are no signs to look for before the Day of the Lord begins.

If these nine characteristics are, in fact, part of the Day of the Lord, there should be evidence in the Old Testament Day of the Lord passages to support this conclusion. Yet, this list does not share any similarity to the first list of the eleven things described in those passages. Comparison of these two lists indicates that they must be *two very distinct periods of time.* So how have pretribulation rapture teachers lumped the tribulation events in with those of the Day of the Lord, then claimed they combine to make up God's wrath? This is hermeneutically unjustifiable. All nine of these important events of the tribulation are absent from or even in contradiction with how the Day of the Lord is portrayed in the Old Testament.

If the two time periods — the tribulation and the Day of the Lord — were one and the same, you would expect the unique and globally significant "tribulation" conditions to be seen in the Old Testament Day of the Lord passages somewhere, but they aren't. In these passages, there is no covenant made by Israel. There are no wars between nations, there are no famines, and there is no pestilence mentioned. Instead, there is only God's wrath against His enemies. There is no spiritual deception by false teachers during the Day of the Lord, since everyone recognizes it as the time of God's wrath. There is no human person being exalted to a God-like position, who is known as the Antichrist. During the Day of the Lord, only God is being glorified. Lastly, there is no mass revival of multitudes who believe in Jesus and then become martyrs for Him.

Yet, despite these facts, pretribulation teachers continue to equate the events of the Day of the Lord, God's climactic end-of-the-age wrath, with the events of the Antichrist's persecution during the tribulation. It is biblically consistent to locate these *two separate* periods of time under the larger umbrella of the 70th Week of Daniel, but the Scripture *never intermixes them* during the entirety of those seven years. Like the proverbial phrase "oil and water don't mix," one may try to mix the tribulation with God's wrath, but it cannot be done biblically or logically.

Notes prewrath teacher P. E. Harris:

> There is a serious problem with equating the concept of the great tribulation with the wrath of God. Because these ideas are two different concepts. Predominately the word "tribulation" in Scripture means the wrath of demoniacally inspired unbelievers persecuting the true believers of God. Thus, when authentic Christians are persecuted for their steadfast loyalty to the Savior Jesus Christ, they suffer tribulation… But on the other hand, "wrath" is God punishing the wicked for their sins, especially those who persecute true believers. Therefore, one concept is the wrath of God, and the other, the great tribulation, is the wrath of Satan. Somehow through the writings of John Nelson Darby and C. I. Scofield, these concepts got intermingled and confused.[40]

It is important to be aware of something found in Paul's letters to the Thessalonians that is related to our discussion of the tribulation and God's wrath. The following references make it clear that the Christians in Thessalonica were undergoing much tribulation on account of their faith in Christ. The initial preaching of the gospel by Paul and Silas converted some, in spite of great opposition against the new Christians by both Jews and Gentiles there (see Acts

---

[40] P.E Harris, *"The Trouble with Tribulation,"* article taken from the website Pulpit and Pen, https://pulpitandpen.org/2017/11/09/the-trouble-with-tribulation/

17:1-9). Later, Paul wrote two letters to them that included the following information about the great persecution they were experiencing:

> You also became imitators of us and of the Lord, having received the word *in much tribulation* ... For you became imitators of God's churches in Judea, which are in Christ Jesus: You *suffered* from your own people the same things those churches *suffered* from the Jews ... We sent Timothy to strengthen and encourage you in your faith, so that no one would be unsettled by *these trials*. For you know quite well that we are destined for them. In fact, when we were with you, we kept telling you that *we would be persecuted*. And it turned out that way, as you well know ... among God's churches we boast about your perseverance and faith in all the *persecutions and trials* you are enduring. (1 Thess. 1:6, 2:14-15, 3:2-4; 2 Thess. 1:4, emphasis added)

In the first letter he sent to these Christians, who were experiencing so much suffering at the hands of men, Paul told them that they would not have to experience the wrath of God (1 Thess. 1:10, 5:9). This reinforces this biblical principle: Christians do experience persecution and tribulation that comes from men and Satan, but they will not experience the Day of the Lord's wrath that comes from God. That wrath is intended for punishment of the Antichrist and his followers, not the church. The entire seven years of Daniel's 70th Week *should not be labeled "the tribulation."* Nor should the entire seven years *be understood to be the Day of the Lord's wrath*. Placed one after the other, they together make up Daniel's 70th Week: the time of tribulation first, followed by the rapture, then the Day of the Lord's wrath.

Finally, and very significantly, the Old Testament says *there will be signs before the Day of the Lord starts*. Elijah must come (Mal. 4:5-6) and the cosmic disturbances must occur (Joel 2:30-31, see Appendix 5, page 171, for a full study on the cosmic disturbances). Pretribulation rapture teachers say this cannot be since they hold there are no prophecies that need to be fulfilled before the rapture and the Day of the Lord begins. To be biblically correct, it is necessary to let go of the idea that these two time periods—the time of tribulation and the Day of the Lord's wrath—are one and the same. The circumstances during the tribulation will result in a horrendous time on the earth, but that does not allow one to identify that time period as being God's wrath.

But could pretribulationists be correct? Is there at least a possibility that some passage revealed later in the New Testament equates the tribulation with the Day of the Lord? The next section will investigate that possibility.

The New Testament and "the Day of the Lord"

The initial Day of the Lord passage found in the New Testament is in the second chapter of Acts. It is well known because it contains the incident that Bible teachers recognize as the birth of the New Testament church on the Day of Pentecost. It was then that the apostle Peter preached a sermon containing a reference to a prophecy in Joel 2:28-32. Peter is explaining what just took place as the Holy Spirit was manifested by many people speaking in unknown languages. The passage from Joel also describes some spectacular things that were prophesied to take place:

> I will show wonders in the heavens above and signs
> on the earth below, blood and fire and billows of
> smoke. The sun will be turned to darkness and the
> moon to blood before the coming of the great and
> glorious day of the Lord. (Acts 2:19-20)

Although Peter applied the passage in Joel 2 to the Jews of his time, there is no indication that the universal darkening (or as we have been calling them, the "cosmic disturbances") took place. Neither did any of the other descriptions of the destruction associated with the Day of the Lord given by the Old Testament prophets. It appears that the events that took place in Jerusalem were a *partial fulfillment* of Joel's prophecy. Now that the promised Messiah had made His appearance, the world had entered the last days of this present age. At that time, we saw fulfillment of several Old Testament promises: a new experience with God's Spirit to regenerate their hearts (Eze.

11:19, 18:31, 36:26-28) and a restatement of the promise that "everyone who calls on the name of the Lord will be saved," but with the new name *Jesus* attached (Acts 2:21-22). But as with other "near-far" prophecies in the Bible, certain details were fulfilled at that time, but others will be fulfilled in the future. The other specific details in Joel's prophecy should be understood to have been put on hold. Neither Peter's speech, nor Luke's writing in Acts, make any attempt to change the original Old Testament meaning of what the Day of the Lord will be like when it is totally fulfilled.

A second time it is found in the first epistle to the Thessalonians:

> Now, brothers and sisters, about times and dates we do not need to write to you, for you know very well that the day of the Lord will come like a thief in the night. While people are saying, "Peace and safety," destruction will come on them suddenly as labor pains on a pregnant woman, and they will not escape. But you, brothers and sisters, are not in darkness so that this day should surprise you like a thief. (1 Thess. 5:1-4)

Notice that the arrival of the Day of the Lord will be *a surprise for unbelievers*, but not to Paul's fellow brothers and sisters who are present and experiencing persecution during the tribulation part of Daniel's 70th Week. The use of the expression "the day of the Lord" here does not indicate any change of the Old Testament meaning. In fact, it reinforces how it was previously portrayed as wrath only against God's enemies. Destruction comes quickly, and the objects of that destruction will be unaware: non-Christians who are blindly following the Antichrist and supporting the persecution. This is a different picture than the one portrayed by pretribulation teachers who tell us that all of the 70th Week is the Day of the Lord's wrath. If this were true, the Antichrist and his followers would be rising in power during the very time God is supposedly pouring out His wrath upon His enemies. This would be in direct contradiction, not only to Paul's words here, but also those of Isaiah, who says that "the Lord alone shall be exalted in that day."

Jesus does not exempt His followers from suffering during the 70th Week. In fact, He tells His disciples that the time of tribulation

begins with birth pangs (Matt. 24:8), and the church will be in the
midst of it, just as many of God's children have always been in
tribulation throughout history. Jesus continues on to say that the
final phase of this period of tribulation, at the end of the age, will
become *mega* ("great," Matt. 24:21). But neither of these things
make it God's wrath. The Day of the Lord's wrath comes later, *after
the rapture brings a halt to the great tribulation.* Jesus said, "For the
sake of the elect [the church] those days [of tribulation] will be cut
short" (Matt. 24:21-22, 29-31; 2 Thess. 1:6-10; Rev. 6:12-17). It is
important to understand that Jesus is telling them that the activities
of the great tribulation get shortened, that is they are stopped. The
length of the seven years of the 70th Week does not get cut short.
The persevering followers of Christ who survive will experience
salvation from the tribulation of the Antichrist's wrath and the
unsuspecting non-believers will finally get their sudden well-
deserved punishment of the Day of the Lord's wrath.

In Paul's follow-up letter to the Thessalonians, we have a third usage
of "the Day of the Lord." He becomes more specific in discussing
its arrival here because of false teaching that had entered the church:

> Now, we request you, brethren, with regard to the
> coming of our Lord Jesus Christ and our gathering
> together to Him, that you not be quickly shaken from
> your composure or be disturbed either by a spirit or
> a message or a letter as if from us, to the effect that
> the day of the Lord has come. Let no one in any way
> deceive you, for it will not come unless the apostasy
> comes first, and the man of lawlessness is revealed.
> (2 Thessalonians 2:1-2)

This passage was previously mentioned to refute the idea that the
rapture has no prophecies needing to be fulfilled before it can occur.
But it is brought up again to determine whether there is anything in
the context that would cause us to change our understanding of the
Day of the Lord from the foundational meaning established in the
Old Testament. Once more, there is nothing in this third New
Testament passage that gives any indication that the events of the
tribulation are part of the Day of the Lord. In fact, it supports the
prewrath understanding of persecution by the Antichrist in the

tribulation happening first, followed by the Day of the Lord. Due to the persecution the church was experiencing, Paul is trying to correct the false teaching that they were already in the Day of the Lord. He does this by reminding them (2 Thess. 2:5) that the tribulation/persecution instituted by the Antichrist must come *before* the Day of the Lord. This agrees with what the apostle had just finished saying a few verses earlier in 1:6-10. Precisely, *the afflicters*, who are already present and doing their dirty work, will receive *their affliction* (God's wrath) when Jesus is revealed (2 Thess. 2:7). This is a reference to the rapture. It will stop the one (the affliction during this time of tribulation) and begin the other (God's wrath). This passage does not allow for tribulation (of the saints) and wrath (against God's enemies) to be intertwined over the entire seven years. Nor does it change the meaning of the Day of the Lord from the Old Testament.

The final reference to the Day of the Lord in the New Testament is made by Peter. Once again, it is combined with the "come like a thief" metaphor as we saw earlier in the 1 Thessalonians 5 passage:

> But the day of the Lord will come like a thief, in which the heavens will pass away with a roar and the elements will be destroyed with intense heat, and the earth and its works will be burned up. (2 Pet. 3:10)

As seen previously in the other "thief" passages, the context of 2 Peter 3:1-12 is clearly saying this surprise arrival of the Day of the Lord is on unbelieving scoffers (2 Pet. 3:3). Those people will mock the teaching that Christ is coming back to destroy those who reject God and the world a second time. However, this is not the mindset of watchful believers. This passage is in accord with the Old Testament and reminds the readers of the previous terrible worldwide calamity that came upon the unbelievers and the physical world by the flood. The future sudden destruction will be unexpected by most, the followers of Antichrist, but expected by others, the believers waiting for the return of the true Christ from heaven to spare them from God's wrath. Peter includes another comment in the context where he tells readers:

> "Since all these things are to be destroyed in this way, what sort of people ought you to be in holy conduct

and godliness, looking for and hastening the coming of
the day of God." (2 Peter 3:11-12)

Because of such close proximity to the previous verse's use of "the
day of the Lord," and because the terms "God" and *"Lord"* can be
used interchangeably, it is reasonable to say that both passages are
referring to God's future wrath at the end of this age. It would be
ridiculous for Peter to encourage Christians to "look forward to" or
to "hasten" the persecution of Christians who come to faith during
this time. Mistakenly, those holding the pretribulation rapture
position are forced to this very conclusion since they equate the
tribulation of the 70th Week with the Day of the Lord. The proper
interpretation is that they are to expectantly welcome God's just
punishment of His enemies along with the accompanying
destruction of the present heavens and earth. They know they may
have to experience the persecution of the Antichrist (Jesus taught
that in the Olivet Discourse), but they will escape God's Day-of-the-
Lord wrath by the rapture, which ends this intense time of suffering.
This will be followed by God's reconstruction of the destroyed
world into the new heavens and earth for the blessings of the
millennial kingdom.

The prewrath teaching does not have this problem because it
recognizes the distinction within the 70th Week between the
tribulation which is followed by the Day of the Lord. There is no
indication of persecution or tribulation for followers of Christ during
the Day of the Lord in either the Old or New Testament passages. In
fact, in that all-important 2 Thessalonians 2 passage, Paul says just
the opposite. He is correcting the false report they were beginning
to believe: that in light of the severe persecution they were
experiencing, they were already in the Day of the Lord. Likewise,
in the passages about the tribulation during the seals of Revelation
6, there is no mention of God's wrath on those who follow the
Antichrist. This is because *the seals are not God's wrathful
judgments.* Yet this is what the pretribulation rapture system
teaches. This teaching has led generations of Christians into placing
the rapture/second coming of Christ in the wrong place: *before* the
seven years of Daniel's 70th Week.

Similar Expressions to "the Day of the Lord"

There are other expressions in the New Testament similar to one we have been focusing on: the Day of the Lord. These include "the day of wrath and revelation of the righteous judgment of God," "the day of our Lord Jesus," "the day of Christ," and "the great day of God." Let's look at these expressions in more detail and how they relate to the Day of the Lord.

In Romans Paul mentions the fate of those individuals who are legalistically moral, but are hypocritically judging others. In the context, these words are directed towards unbelievers who have in their minds some ethical standards, but their morals do not measure up to God's righteousness—something the apostle later explains can only be received by faith:

> But because of your stubbornness and unrepentant heart you are storing up wrath for yourself in the day of wrath and revelation of the righteous judgment of God, who will render to every man according to his deeds. (Romans 2:5-6)

The focus on this passage is on the future judgment by God *over all unbelievers* for all time based on their works.[ii] It will take place at the Great White Throne judgment of Revelation 20:11-15 and will result in God's eternal wrath in the "lake of fire," or hell. While the eschatological wrath of the Day of the Lord is temporary and takes place just before the establishment of the millennial kingdom, God's wrathful lake of fire punishment for unbelievers begins after the millennium and goes on for eternity.

There are three times in his letters to the Corinthians, Paul also uses the expression "the day of our Lord Jesus":

1. 1 Corinthians 1:7-8: "eagerly awaiting the revelation of our Lord Jesus Christ, who will confirm you to the end, blameless in the day of our Lord Jesus Christ."

2. 1 Corinthians 5:5: "I have decided to deliver such a one to Satan for the destruction of his flesh, that his spirit may be saved in the day of the Lord Jesus."

3. 2 Corinthians 1:14: "We are your reason to be proud as you are ours in the day of our Lord Jesus."

These are eschatological passages, but in each, the context is on Christians being in the presence of Jesus after His return and without any hint of God's judgment, wrath, or destruction. There is nothing in any of these passages that would change the meaning the Day of the Lord from being God's judgment destined for the unbelievers on earth after the tribulation.

In Philippians, Paul uses an eschatological expression, "the day of Christ [Jesus]," three times:

1. Philippians 1:6: "For I am confident of this very thing, that He who began a good work in you will perfect it until the day of Christ Jesus."

2. Philippians 1:10: "So that you may approve the things that are excellent, in order to be sincere and blameless until the day of Christ."

3. Philippians 2:16: "Holding fast the word of life, so that in the day of Christ I will have reason to glory because I did not run in vain nor toil in vain."

Just like in the Corinthians passages, these three verses are talking about a judgment of Christians only, most likely in the presence of Jesus at His judgment seat in order to give rewards to them (Rom. 14:10, 1 Cor. 3:10-15, 2 Cor. 5:10). These expressions have nothing to do with the Day of the Lord's wrath, so they have no impact on our understanding of that term.

The final passage a similar expression is found is:

> For they are spirits of demons, performing signs, which go out to the kings of the whole world, to gather them together for the war of *the great day of God, the Almighty*. (Rev. 16:14, emphasis added)

The context is in the future with John's vision of the sixth and seventh bowl judgments. Almost all would agree that all the bowls are a part of the Day of the Lord's wrath. But this appears to be referring to a final climax of that wrath called the Battle of Armageddon (Rev. 16:16). It will take place at the end (or immediately after) Daniel's 70ᵗʰ Week when the leaders of the nations will gather their forces outside of Jerusalem to resist Christ's enthronement as King. Their plans are thwarted when they are destroyed by God's supernatural intervention. They will receive these final bowl judgments, which complete the God's Day-of-the-Lord wrath. This verse agrees nicely with the Old Testament's depiction of the Day of the Lord, which is only God judgments on earth against those who oppose Him.

All of these expressions from the New Testament, though similar to the translation "Day of the Lord," do not provide justification for adjusting the original definition derived from the Old Testament passages.

Summary of 'the Day of the Lord'

The foundation of how we should understand the Day of the Lord is clearly laid in the Old Testament. It is the destruction of all those who reject God, along with the demolition of the present heavens and earth. The persecution during the tribulation, which will be experienced by all who do not follow the Antichrist and false prophet, is an expression of Satan's wrath, not God's. To be mistaken about the identity of the Day of the Lord will lead to the incorrect location of the rapture. If the first five seals of the tribulation are not God's wrath, then *the rapture does not have to happen before they take place.* Therefore, the rapture is not imminent at that time since the church will experience those events. As Paul clearly states, the Day of the Lord will come *after* the apostasy and *after* the Antichrist is revealed, which are the most significant events of the tribulation, according to Jesus and Paul. The tribulation and the Day of the Lord's wrath are *two distinct prophetic periods*, even though they both fall within Daniel's 70ᵗʰ Week. The tribulation is first, which is cut short by the rapture sometime after the abomination of desolation. This is then followed immediately by God's wrath on the unbelievers who remain on earth after the rapture. There will be a remnant of Jews and Gentiles who reject the Antichrist and will be protected during God's wrath just like the prophets in the Old Testament mentioned. They will come to faith later and enter into Christ's millennial kingdom in order to repopulate the earth after God's wrath is complete.[iii]

The prewrath interpretation is the most consistent with the Old and New Testament passages that mention the expression the Day of the Lord.

What About Jesus Removing the Seals from the Scroll?

Most rapture teachers agree that the first five seals of the scroll in Revelation 6:1-11 correspond to the tribulation events described in the Olivet Discourse in Matthew 24:3-28. Pretribulationists claim, however, that since Jesus is removing the seals, He is causing the events and therefore they must be God's wrath.

As described by Dr. Richard Schmidt:

> Jesus will methodically unroll the scroll, removing one of the seven seals at a time until the scroll is fully open. Each of the seven seals symbolically represent literal horrific judgments that the inhabitants of the earth will face.[41]

Dr. John MacArthur agrees:

> The chronology is very clear, the first four seals occur in the front part, the first three and a half [years], they are the ones Jesus called the beginning of the birth pains, they happen in the first part. This fifth seal begins in the first part, stretches across the midpoint, is accelerated in the second part, and is followed by the vengeance… So, we're looking at the beginning of this judgment, in this time of wrath. It is delineated, as I said, through these seven seals.[42]

Do you see the important word "judgments" used to describe the

---

[41] Dr. Richard Schmidt, *"The First and Second Seal Judgments,"* https://dispensationalpublishing.com/the-first-and-second-seal-judgments-the-white-and-red-horses/ (last accessed 8/21/19).

[42] Dr. John MacArthur, *"God's Great Day of Wrath, the Fifth Seal of Revelation 6:9-11"* (sermon: November 15, 1992) https://www.gty.org/library/sermons-library/66-25/gods-great-day-of-wrath (last accessed 8/21/19).

seals? If all seven seals are God's judgments, then one is forced to conclude that the fifth seal is the result of God's wrath, too. However, the breaking of the fifth seal indicates the martyrdom of multitudes of God's own disciples. It is important to carefully evaluate this seal rather than jump to the conclusion, "This is so terrible that a bunch of people have been martyred. See? This is so bad that it proves that God's wrath is taking place." This is what pretribulationists do.

Carefully read this critical passage before interpreting it:

> And when the Lamb opened the fifth seal, I saw under the altar the souls of those who had been slain for the word of God and for the testimony they had upheld. And they cried out in a loud voice, "How long, O Lord, *until You judge those who live on the earth and avenge our blood*?" Then each of them was given a white robe and told to rest a little while longer, until the full number of their fellow servants, their brothers, were killed, just as they had been killed. (Rev. 6:9-11, emphasis added)

If this seal is part of God's Day of the Lord, then *Christians are being slaughtered by God's wrath!* In fact, the pretribulationist's supposed wrath of God is not completed until more followers of Jesus are killed. This interpretation is in direct contradiction to Paul's statements about the church missing God's wrath (1 Thess. 1:10, 5:9). The prewrath view, that these seals are describing the tribulation and not God's wrath, coincides with all of Christ's Olivet Discourse and Paul's letters to the Thessalonians. An important aspect of the sinful human condition that began with Cain and Able is being multiplied exponentially at the fifth seal in the last days: God's allowance of the persecution of the righteous by the unrighteous, even to the extent of murder. This persecution is the consequence of His sovereign permissive plan, not the result of His intentional wrath. Here are three biblical illustrations of this:

1. Joseph after his mistreatment by his brothers: "As for you, you meant evil against me, but God meant it for good in order to bring about this present result." (Gen. 50:20)

2. Satan being given permission to wreck Job's physical life: "Then the Lord said to Satan, 'Behold, all that he has is in your power, only do not put forth your hand on him.'" (Job 1:12)

3. Jesus' death on the cross: "This man, delivered up by the predetermined plan and foreknowledge of God; you nailed to a cross by the hands of godless men and put Him to death." (Acts 2:23)

The Bible never calls these and other situations like them results of God's wrath. Likewise, Christ's removal of the seals does not establish that He is causing the effects that they represent. Does He foreknow that these evil things would happen? Yes. Can we say that He permitted them to happen? Yes. Everything in these examples will be repeated in the experiences of Christians, *even during the terrible time of tribulation of the seals*. God's children have been going through these things throughout human history. They come at the hand of fallen angelic and/or sinful human beings. The ultimate climax will take place while God's people are persecuted during the seals in the tribulation under the final and ultimate Antichrist.

The wrath of God, which arrives later, is clearly differentiated from the seals. God's wrath comes during the trumpets and bowls, which are administered by angels. Did you notice? The trumpets and bowls are directed by angels, while the seals are not. This is a very important distinction. The trumpets and bowls are managed by God's holy angels, who take their orders directly from Him. Unfortunately, this distinction is not recognized by pretribulationists who have grouped the seals, trumpet and bowls together as God's wrath.

The better interpretation of this, and consistent with many biblical examples, is that the removal of the seals by Jesus implies His sovereign *permission of these evil actions*. Paul expresses this theological principle of God's permissive will in a very popular verse: "We know that God works all things together for the good of those who love Him, who are called according to His purpose" (Rom. 8:28). This verse must be understood in light of the entire context of Romans 8:16-39, which deals with the question of why

Christians are allowed to suffer as a part of God's loving plan being acted out in human history. The apostle assures believers that their suffering is for the purpose of experiencing greater eternal glory in heaven if they endure it (Rom. 8:17-18, 30). We are told that God is for us and not against us (Rom. 8:31) and that nothing can separate us from His love (Rom. 8:35-39).

Orthodox Christian theology has always understood that somehow God is mysteriously *allowing* all events to take place, but He is not the one responsible for *causing* the behavior of the unrighteous ones (James 1:12-15). The martyrdom of Christians that will occur during this time of tribulation is not from God, instead we see that it comes from Satan:

> Then I heard a loud voice in heaven, saying, "Now the salvation, and the power, and the kingdom of our God and the authority of His Christ have come, for the accuser of our brethren has been thrown down … And they overcame him because of the blood of the Lamb and because of the word of their testimony, and they did not love their life even when faced with death. For this reason, rejoice, O heavens and you who dwell in them. Woe to the earth and the sea, because *the devil has come down to you, having great wrath,* knowing that he has only a short time." (Revelation 12:10-12, emphasis added)

From the earthly perspective, the tribulation is a time of woe for those who will experience the wrath of Satan. It is not wrath from God. These martyrs are said to be overcoming Satan, because ultimately their deaths will glorify Jesus, and they will be rewarded for it. Later John says these Christian martyrs are said to be blessed:

> And I heard a voice from heaven, saying, "Write, 'Blessed are the dead who die in the Lord from now on!' Yes, so that they may rest from their labors, for their deeds follow with them," says the Spirit. (Revelation 14:13)

Beginning with the murders of Abel and all of the Old Testament prophets, until the final righteous martyr's death in the tribulation (see Matthew 23:34-37 and Revelation 6:11), the blame is always placed on sinful people, not God's wrath. God's permission of persecution of the righteous is totally different from His punishing wrath against His unbelieving enemies.

Seals Are Different from the Trumpets and Bowls

Besides not seeing the different sources of the seals and the trumpets and bowls, pretribulationists do not recognize the difference between the characteristics of the seals of Revelation 6 and the trumpets and bowls of Revelation 8. The first five seals represent events similar to those that have been occurring throughout human history. War, poverty, famine, pestilence, evil rulers, martyrdom, and natural disasters are the consequences of the sinful condition of the world in general. However, when the sixth seal opens, we see supernatural heavenly changes in the sun, moon, and stars, which were foreshadowed in the Old Testament. Recall that this unique combination of cosmic disturbances was said by Jesus to happen *after* the time of tribulation (Matt. 24:29), but *before* the Day of the Lord (Joel 2:31). Once the seventh seal is removed later in Revelation 8:1, these last two groups of seven metaphors, the trumpets and bowls, will deliver God's wrath. Until then, His wrath is held back by angels (Rev. 7:1-3) until the completion of two events: the sealing of 144,000 Jews (7:4-8) and the appearance of a large multitude of people who come out of the great tribulation (7:9-17).

This series of events is also strong support of the distinction between the tribulation of the saints and God's "soon to arrive" wrath upon unbelievers. The parallel with the Olivet Discourse is obvious since the time of tribulation will be "cut short" (Matt. 24:21-22) at the appearing of Jesus and the gathering of the elect (Matt. 24:29-31). This gathering/rapture corresponds to the sudden appearing of the multitudes worshipping in heaven, recorded in Revelation 7:9-17 after the sixth seal appearance of Jesus in the clouds. The elder specifically says the multitude who suddenly show up in heaven "came out of the great tribulation" (Rev. 7:14). Notice also, the sixth seal appearance of Christ is followed immediately by the recognition of God's wrath about to come upon the ungodly people of the world. These people see Jesus on His glorious throne and know what is about to happen. This causes them to cry out, "The great day of their wrath has come!" and "Who is able to stand?" (Rev. 6:14-17). The interpretation most consistent with these passages is that the tribulation of the saints is contained in the first five seals, and it ends when the universe goes dark and is followed by Jesus appearing to gather His elect into heaven. At this point, the unbelievers remaining on the earth realize God's wrath is about to hit them. Then the angels will carry out God's Day of the Lord judgments indicated by the trumpets and bowls.

The Day of Their Wrath "Has Come"

One of the watershed passages related to the timing of the rapture deals with the sixth seal and the interpretation of the statement "the day of their wrath *has come*" in Revelation 6:17. A disagreement centers around the exact meaning of the Greek aorist tense of the verb. The Greek word *ēlthen* is the aorist of the verb *erchomai* and is translated *has come* or *is come* in almost every major English version of Revelation 6:17. There is no debate over the meaning of the word as shown by the consensus in using the English word "come." The difficulty is in interpreting the timing of this "coming" of God's wrath.

One understanding is that this is referring to wrath that *started some time in the past and is continuing*. Pretribulationists take it that way and say that God's wrath began with the first seal and continues through the remaining seals, as well as the trumpets and the bowls that follow. Since they say His wrath begins with the first seal, they argue that the rapture must take place before it at the beginning of Daniel's 70th Week. Prewrath teachers, on the other hand, understand the aorist tense here as being futuristic. They understand this wrath as *about to happen*. It will arrive sometime after this proclamation is made at the sixth seal, so the church does not have to be raptured before all of the previous seals. Because of the significance of the interpretation of this single verb, it will be dealt with in some detail. Let's first read the context of this verse in Revelation 6 before discussing the details:

> And I looked when He broke the sixth seal, and there
> was a great earthquake; and the sun became black as
> sackcloth made of hair, and the whole moon became
> like blood; and the stars of the sky fell to the earth,
> as a fig tree casts its unripe figs when shaken by a
> great wind. And the sky was split apart like a scroll
> when it is rolled up; and every mountain and island
> were moved out of their places. And the kings of the
> earth and the great men and the commanders and the
> rich and the strong and every slave and free man hid
> themselves in the caves and among the rocks of the
> mountains; and they said to the mountains and the
> rocks, "Fall on us and hide us from the presence of
> Him who sits on the throne *and from the wrath of the
> Lamb; for the great day of their wrath has come*; and
> who is able to stand?" (Rev. 6:12-17, emphasis mine)

The aorist tense in Greek is open ended because the time and the action of the verb is often described as *indefinite* or *undefined*. This means the aorist tense does not specifically tell us the time or kind of the action taking place. We are attempting to discern the time when God's wrath begins to take place since that affects where we locate the rapture. Does the aorist in Revelation 6:17 infer wrath that has been going on in the past? This meaning is often labeled as the *constative* nuance and is favored by the pretribulation teachers. Prewrath interpreters prefer the *ingressive* or *proleptic* nuance, which focuses on a soon beginning of God's judgments. Thus, from the prewrath view, the better translation is with a future nuance: "the wrath of God is about to come."[iv] That said, the following information will attempt to show that the *ingressive* or *proleptic* is the preferred nuance and that Revelation 6:17 should be understood as "the wrath that is about to take place."

When Is the First Indication of God's Wrath?

First, it should be pointed out that Revelation 6:17, at the sixth seal, is the first time the word "wrath" is used in Revelation. If the first five seals are God's wrath, as pretribulationists believe, would it not make sense that "wrath," or some word with similar meaning, would be used somewhere during that time? The world events are terrible, but there is no indication that they are God's direct punishment for mankind's sin. Interestingly, God is asked by the martyrs of the fifth seal who are under the throne, "How long will You refrain from avenging our blood on those who dwell on the earth?" (Rev. 6:10). This request implies that the cause of their deaths is not God's wrath, but the hatred of people who dwell on the earth. Not only do followers of Jesus not experience His wrath, but in answer to the martyrs' question, God tells them that He will eventually fulfill their request sometime *in the future* (Rev. 6:11). This tells us that, at this point in the fifth seal, He has not yet been demonstrating His wrath.

Who Is Saying "the Wrath of God Has Come?"

Second, we need to carefully look at who is speaking at the sixth seal when they say, "The great day of their wrath has come" (rather, is coming). Significantly, it is not the apostle John, or an angel, or one of the 24 elders, or one of the four creatures, or God Himself. John is repeating the words of those who have been alive during the events of Daniel's 70th Week. These people are now attempting to hide themselves from God's wrath (reread Isaiah 2:12-21), which they recognize *is about to come upon them.* The text says there is a great earthquake, then the world goes completely dark as a result of the cosmic disturbances. Recall the time references with respect to these unique prophesied events: *after* the tribulation (Matt. 24:29) and *before* the Day of the Lord (Joel 2:10, 30-31). These people's experience of global "lights out" precedes the sight of a bright light as the sky opens up and the glorified Son of God appears.

Who is seeing these things and then responding to them? I am in complete agreement with one of my former professors, who said this:

> The nations of the earth have been deceived by the false teaching of the harlot system (Revelation 14:8) and have partaken of the "wine of her fornication." They have followed the false prophet in the worship of the beast (Revelation 13:11-18). For this godlessness the nations must be judged. This

judgment comes on "the kings of the earth, and the
great men, and the rich men, and the chief captains,
and the mighty men, and on every slave and free…"
(Revelation 6:15), all of whom "blasphemed the
name of God …and they repented not to give Him
Glory" (Revelation 16:9). — J. Dwight Pentecost[43]

This group in Revelation 6:12-17 are the ungodly who have been
carrying out the Antichrist's persecutions during the tribulation and
exalting his name even to the point of worshipping him. But
remember Isaiah 2:17 said "the Lord alone will be exalted" during
the Day of the Lord. What they have been doing to their victims
around the world cannot be God's wrath, since His wrath is intended
only for the enemies of Christ, not His disciples. In light of their
description as being kings, great and rich, chief captains, and mighty
men, it appears that they have not been the recipients of the negative
effects of the tribulation. Rather, they likely are the supporters and
some even the leaders of those atrocities. The events of the first five
seals can easily be attributed to the consequences of humans.
Nothing in Revelation 6:1-11 indicates that God is supernaturally
imposing His wrath to punish His enemies. It does not make sense
that these people now attempting to hide have been experiencing
God's wrath. Instead, to their great shock, they see the appearance
of the glory of Jesus Christ and they know that God's wrath is about
to hit them hard.[44]

Sinners Know They Are About to Meet an Angry God

As Jesus appears in the sky at the sixth seal, observe the reaction of

---

[43] J. Dwight Pentecost, *Things to Come*, 238-239.

[44] Recall in Acts 9 where we see some interesting similarities to what will happen
at the sixth seal. Saul has been persecuting the Christians when Jesus suddenly
appears to him in a bright light and proclaims in Acts 9:4-5, "Saul, Saul, why have
you been persecuting Me? I am Jesus whom you are persecuting." The persecution
of Christ's followers is the same as persecuting the Lord Jesus Himself. The same
will be true during the great tribulation as the Antichrist's followers will be
persecuting those who refuse to follow him just before Jesus returns in His glory
at the sixth seal.

these people after realizing they are *suddenly* in the presence of the glorified Jesus Christ. They are seeking any place to escape, looking even for caves and pleading for rocks to fall on them. Also, take note of their words:

> And they said to the mountains and the rocks, "Fall on us and hide us from the presence of Him who sits on the throne and from the wrath of the Lamb, for the great day of their wrath has come." (Rev. 6:16-17)

This is hardly a casual observation that God's wrath has been going on for a period of time. Wouldn't they already have recognized the presence of God's wrath in the previous seals? We would certainly expect that to be the case. But the truth is, the tribulation of the saints depicted in the first five seals, for which these people will be responsible, is not God's wrath. They are the ones who are caught by surprise—*like a thief in the night*. However, that is not how the pretribulation rapture teachers interpret this passage. They claim the first five seals are God's punishing judgments. Explains one pretribulation rapture teacher (emphasis mine):

> Their hiding *is not anticipatory, but reactionary.* In other words, the events of the sixth seal are part of the Day of the Lord. The reaction of the unbelieving world to the terrors unleashed by the sixth seal will not be one of repentance but of mindless panic. *They will finally acknowledge what believers have been saying all along, that the disasters they have experienced are God's judgment.* — Dr. Tony Garland[45]

This statement misses the point of what God is revealing in these verses about the sixth seal. The reaction of these people *is anticipatory*. The terror they exhibit clearly shows that they recognize that the tables are about to be turned on them. The tribulation, caused by the Antichrist, which they have been promoting against the righteous people, has come to a screeching

---

[45] Dr. Tony Garland,
https://www.biblestudytools.com/Bible/OurLibrary/Commentaries/ATestimony ofJesusChrist/Revelation6/Revelation 6:17, 12/4/18.

halt. Now God's wrath *is about to come* very quickly on them, just as Paul told the Thessalonians:

> While people are saying, 'Peace and safety,' destruction will come on them suddenly, as labor pains on a pregnant woman, and they will not escape (1 Thess. 5:3, NIV).

Some interpret this to mean that there is peace and safety in the world during this time, but that is not what this verse says. At that time, peace and safety *is the goal* of these people under Antichrist's rule. What they are striving for—peace and safety—seems, in their own minds, to be a noble cause.[v] But how many times in history have there been groups of people who attempt to bring peace and safety to the world, then end up resorting to violence and murder to get rid of anyone who disagrees with them? These future followers of Antichrist will do the same, only to the greatest extent than ever before by other antichrists. They will become afflicters of those who reject his plan, which is ultimately to get the world to honor and worship him as God. However, it will not be long until they receive God's righteous punishment for their evil actions. This lines up perfectly with what Paul says in his second letter to the Thessalonians:

> For after all it is only just for God to repay with affliction those who afflict you, and to give relief to you who are afflicted and to us as well when the Lord Jesus will be revealed from heaven with His mighty angels in flaming fire, dealing out retribution to those who do not know God and to those who do not obey the gospel of our Lord Jesus. (2 Thess. 1:6-8)

Based on all of the information, it is not accurate to claim that God's wrath has been present during the first five seals. When the unbelievers see Christ, they are struck with terror, and their words indicate that His punishment of them, the Day of the Lord, is right around the corner—soon to arrive, very soon!

What About Other "Futuristic" Aorist Verbs?

A third reason to support the best translation of Revelation 6:17 as

God's wrath "is about to come" is because of other instances where aorist verbs have a futuristic meaning. We are going to see other examples of aorist tenses in the book of Revelation, including some with the same Greek verb *ēlthen,* which was used in Revelation 6:17. Below are several more found in Revelation showing that futuristic aorist verbs are not as rare as some pretribulation rapture teachers think. It is important to look closely at the context of each use in order to determine the nuance. One should not just depend on the English words such as "has come" or "has been," which many translations have chosen to use.

> **1. Revelation 10:7 (NIV):** "But in the days when the seventh angel is *about to sound* his trumpet, the mystery of God *will be accomplished* [aorist of verb "to complete," or "to fulfill"], just as he announced to his servants the prophets" (emphasis mine).

This aorist verb is understood by the NIV translators and others as *proleptic/future,* since it reads that the mystery *will be* accomplished. The reason is that the preliminary sounding of the trumpet is "about to sound." This justifies the meaning of the accomplishment of the mystery of God's will as being futuristic.

> **2. Revelation 11:14-15:** "The second woe is past; behold, the third woe *is coming quickly.* Then the seventh angel sounded; and there were loud voices in heaven, saying, 'The kingdom of the world *has become* [aorist of "to become"] the kingdom of our Lord and of His Christ; and He *will reign* [future tense of "to rule"] forever and ever." (emphasis added)

Since the second woe has passed, but God's judgment of the third woe "is coming quickly," clearly the third woe is yet future. The seventh angel's trumpet sounds and there are voices giving details about this woe, *which will take place in the future.* Most English versions of 11:15 have the aorist of "to become" translated as the past completed action "has become." If you are depending on the English words without closely examining the context, however, you will miss either the ingressive nuance "is about to become" or the proleptic "will become." There are two good contextual reasons for this perspective. First, at that time of this future third woe, the kingdom of the world *will not yet have become* the kingdom of Jesus, since the wrath of God must first be completed. Second, the next clause has a future tense: "He *will reign* forever." His millennial reign will only begin in the future, after God finishes His wrath. A superior translation of this announcement is, "The kingdom of the world *is about to become* [or *"will become"*] the kingdom of Christ, and then He will reign forever" (emphasis mine).

One pretribulation rapture teacher is convinced this is a futuristic aorist (he calls it "prophetic") in his commentary on Revelation. Here is what he says about the aorist of the Greek word *ginomai* in Revelation 11:15:

> "Have become": ἐγένετο [*egeneto*], singular, prophetic aorist. The event is so certain in the sending of the seventh angel that it is treated as if already past. However, the kingdom will not have arrived in totality until all seven bowl judgments are poured forth and the King Himself returns to earth to defeat the armies of the nations." — Dr. Tony Garland[46]

For further discussion on this topic, see the related endnote[vi].

> **3. Revelation 11:16-17 (NIV):** "And the twenty-four elders, who were seated on their thrones before God, fell on their faces and worshiped God, saying: 'We give thanks to you, Lord God Almighty, the One who is and who was, because you have taken your great power and *have begun to reign*' [aorist of "to rule or to reign"]" (emphasis added).

This passage is a continuation of the previous two verses just discussed in Revelation 11:14-15. The aorist of the verb "to rule" should be interpreted in light of the context, with the same word in verse 15, which says there will be a future ruling by Jesus. The action of Christ's reign is either just beginning (ingressive) or it is

---

[46] Dr. Tony Garland,
www.spiritandtruth.org/teaching/Book_of_Revelation/commentary/htm/chapters/11.html#3.11.15.

in the future (proleptic). The point is that the action of the aorist does not mean that Christ's ruling has been going on in the past.

> **4. Revelation 14:6-8, 18:2:** Then I saw another angel flying in midair, and he had the eternal gospel to proclaim to those who live on the earth—to every nation, tribe, language and people. He said in a loud voice, "Fear God and give him glory, because the hour of his judgment *has come*" [aorist: *ēlthen*]...A second angel followed and said, "*Fallen, fallen* [both are aorist] is Babylon the great, which made all the nations drink the maddening wine of her adulteries"...And he cried out in a mighty voice saying, "*Fallen, fallen* [again, both are aorist verbs] is Babylon the great!" (emphasis added)

In these passages, the first aorist, *ēlthen,* is also translated "has come," just as in Revelation 6:17. But a future nuance is likely because the proclamation of the gospel to the whole world through the angel would be followed by God's future judgment. The statement about the fall of Babylon is translated as a past action, but should be understood as a future event in light of the details of that judgment given about it in Revelation 16:17-19:3.[vii]

> **5. Revelation 14:15:** "Then another angel came out of the temple and called in a loud voice to him who was sitting on the cloud, 'Take your sickle and reap, because the time to reap *has come* [*ēlthen*], for the harvest of the earth *is ripe*'" (emphasis mine).

Again, an angel uses the same verbal expression as in Revelation 6:17 and 14:8. This one is talking about a reaping that is just now beginning or is in the future. It was not possible in the past, but it is now. The context clearly implies that the time to reap has just recently been entered. Previously, the time was not right. Also, no reaping could occur earlier since the reaper did not have his sickle. Once he takes up the tool, the reaping will begin.

> **6. Revelation 19:6-9 (NIV):** Then I *heard* [aorist] something like the voice of a great multitude and like the sound of many waters and like the sound of mighty

peals of thunder, saying, 'Hallelujah! For the Lord our God, the Almighty *reigns* [aorist]. Let us rejoice and be glad and give the glory to Him, for the marriage of the Lamb *has come* [aorist: *ēlthen*] and His bride *has prepared* [aorist] herself.' It *was given* [aorist] to her to clothe herself in fine linen, bright and clean; for the fine linen is the righteous acts of the saints. Then he said to me, "Write, 'Blessed are those who are invited to the marriage supper of the Lamb.'" (emphasis added)

This passage contains five aorist verbs. Recall that since the time of action of the aorist is undefined, there are a variety of nuances to consider. This is an example of how the context and the verb itself determine when the action takes place.

The context of Revelation 19:1-10 is a celebration of worship in heaven after the seventh bowl of wrath has been poured out and the mysterious harlot city Babylon has been destroyed. Jesus is either already reigning or is about to begin reigning in His earthly kingdom. There is another aorist, *ēlthen,* in Revelation 19:7, which, again, is translated by the NASB as a past action: "the marriage of the Lamb *has come*." As usual, this obscures the better futuristic understanding; therefore, the translation should be, "the marriage of the Lamb is about to take place." This is most likely because the invitations have been received and the bride has made herself ready. If the marriage supper was presently going on, it would likely read: "Blessed are those who are attending" instead of "are invited."

Conclusion About Revelation 6:17

The impact of how one interprets the words spoken in Revelation 6:17 on the timing of the rapture cannot be overemphasized. The issue we have spent a lot of time considering is what is meant by "the day of their wrath *has come*." As these unbelievers are desperately looking for a place to hide from God's presence, does the aorist of the verb "to come" mean His wrath has already been going on (pretribulation interpretation)? Or, does the ingressive or futuristic nuance of the Greek aorist tense apply (the prewrath understanding)? If the latter is the case, then they are stating that God's wrath is about to begin soon in the future. With the aorist, either of these are possible. The deciding factor is which meaning fits best in the overall context of the six seals up to this point. The state of affairs in the world during this time was discussed. If the first five seals are God's wrath, then can it be possible that His wrath is responsible for the deaths of so many Christians? If the first five seals are God's wrath, why is it only then that the unbelievers acknowledge this fact, and they start seeking protection at the sixth seal? Good answers to these questions must be given. Readers must be the judge as to whether the pretribulation or the prewrath rapture interpretation best fits the context. It was also mentioned that the first usage of the word "wrath" in the book of Revelation is found twice in this verse about the sixth seal. Six other aorist verbs in Revelation were examined, some being the exact same verb, showing that the futuristic meaning of the aorist tense in Revelation 6:17 is actually not a rare occurrence.

To conclude this section, I will quote Charles Cooper, with whose summary of Revelation 6:17 I wholeheartedly agree:

> Please show me where in Revelation 6:17 one can get the evidence to say that the wrath of God is involved in seals one through five... The wicked are running to hide from the Throne-Sitter and the Lamb. If the wrath of God has been falling beginning with seal one, why are the wicked—six seals later—just beginning to run and hide? If seals one though six are the wrath of God, the wicked do not know it... The Greek language in Revelation 6:17 supports the conclusion that the wrath of God is imminent but still has not actually begun, which is precisely why the wicked are trying to find a hiding place. In the Greek language an aorist verb can indicate an action is just beginning (ingressive); an action has been going on for a long time (historical); an action just happens without emphasis on when it will happen (gnomic); and several other options are possible. It is clear that based upon the actions of the wicked, an ingressive

aorist is the correct usage in Revelation 6:17. The wrath of God is imminent, but it has not yet begun.[47]

For more on this, see Appendix 1 (page 137, "The Rapture in the Book of Revelation?").

---

[47] Charles Cooper, *A Pre-Wrath Response to 'Fatal Flaws in the Modern Pre-Wrath Rapture Position,'* conspiracyclothes.com/nowheretorun/a-pre-wrath-response-to-fatal-flaws-in-the-modern-pre-wrath-rapture-position-by-charles-cooper/, December 4, 2018.

[i] The Problem with Two 'Second Comings' of Christ

A detail in Mr. Kreider's quotation illustrates a point of confusion created by the pretribulation rapture teaching. It concerns the expressions "the return of Christ" (or as others who hold to the pretribulation rapture positions call it, "the coming of Christ at the end of Daniel's 70th Week). The Greek word under discussion here is *parousia,* which can mean the "initial arrival" or possibly "presence after arriving." It is important to be aware that *parousia* is translated as "coming" in clear passages that are talking about the rapture (see below). The same word is also found in other passages describing Christ's second coming to the earth in power and glory, which pretribulation rapture teachers say takes place seven years later. Many refuse to call the rapture His "return" or "second coming" because they say Jesus does not actually come to the earth at that time. He simply meets the saints in the sky, then goes back to heaven. Instead, they reserve the English expression "coming" only for His return at the end of the seven years. This is illustrated in the following statements (emphasis added):

> At the rapture, Jesus comes for His saints, at *the Second Coming* He comes with His saints. — Dr. David Jeremiah (*What Is the Difference between the Rapture and the Second Coming?* Crosswalk.com.)

> At *the end of the Tribulation* Jesus Christ will return…At *this second coming* the Antichrist will be cast into the Lake of Fire and Satan will be bound for a thousand years. (*The Second Coming of Christ,* https://www.MoodyBible.org, July 4, 2019)

The first problem with this understanding is that Jesus and Paul both use the Greek word *parousia* to describe the rapture:

> But of that day and hour, no one knows, not even the angels in heaven, nor the Son, but the Father alone. For the coming [*parousia*] of the Son of Man will be just like the Days of Noah… so shall the coming [*parousia*] of the Son of Man be." (Matt. 24:36-39)

> For who is our hope or joy or crown of exultation? Is it not even you, in the presence of our Lord Jesus at His coming [*parousia*] …So that He may establish your hearts unblameable in holiness before our God and Father at the coming [*parousia*] of our Lord Jesus with all His saints…For this we say to you by the word of the Lord, that we who are alive, and remain until the coming [*parousia*] of the Lord shall not precede those who have fallen asleep. (1 Thess. 2:19, 3:13, 4:15)

> Now we request you, brethren, with regard to the coming [*parousia*] of our Lord Jesus Christ, and our gathering together to Him. (2 Thess. 2:1)

These are clearly rapture passages and not a Second Coming or return to earth that concludes Daniel's 70th Week, according to their scenarios. These pretribulation teachers tell us *the rapture is not Christ's coming*, even though the same word is used for both. Is this done based on good exegetical and lexical evidence? Or is it derived because they must keep the church out of the tribulation? The best answer is the latter.

By splitting up Christ's coming (*parousia*) into two separate events separated by seven years, this creates another problem. They claim that nobody knows when Jesus will "come/return at the rapture [*parousia*], but at the same time, they define His "return*"* [*parousia*] as His glorious coming to earth at the end of seven years of tribulation. If their definition of "coming/return" is true, then we would be able to know the day it will occur since it would be exactly seven years after Israel and the Antichrist make the covenant. They cannot have it both ways. They cannot split up Christ's *parousia* into two distinct second comings, then tell us that the rapture is not His "coming," even though the Bible says it is, and then say we do not know when His second "coming" [*parousia*] will happen. This is confusing unless you force *parousia* to mean what it does not mean and split it into two separate events, as well as wrongly identify the tribulation with God's wrath.

Other pretribulationists will disagree with their pretribulation rapture brethren who hold to the above definition that only the "end of the tribulation glorious return" is Christ's second coming. This group will acknowledge the rapture as His "coming" [*parousia*] and also call the glorious appearance the Second Coming, too. When they do this, they create the problem of having two Second Comings, thus making a total of three "comings" of Christ in all. The first was His physical birth and earthly life. His first Second Coming is at the rapture (remember, *parousia* is used in the rapture passages of Matthew 24:36-39; 1 Thessalonians 4:15; 2 Thessalonians 2:1). The second Second Coming in glory is at the end of the tribulation to destroy His enemies they say is depicted in Revelation 19:11-21.

Some other pretribulationists will disagree with these semantics. They attempt to avoid this problem by claiming that the two uses of *parousia,* at the beginning and the end the seven years of Daniel's 70th Week, are *two aspects* of a single Second Coming. For details of this understanding, see Dr. Charles Ryrie's explanation in *What You Should Know About the Rapture,* p. 44. Dr. Dwight Pentecost also goes to great lengths to explain this distinction on pp. 206-207 in his book *Things to Come,* even though he acknowledged on p. 157 that *parousia* is used for both the non-glorious rapture and the glorious coming at the end of Daniel's 70th Week. Note that, in the original quotation, Kreider says that the Day of the Lord will precede His return, so by "return," he means Christ's coming in power and glory after the seven-year tribulation/Day of the Lord is completed, and not the imminent rapture/Second Coming. Kreider is in agreement with what Ryrie and Pentecost.

The prewrath teaching avoids this confusion by seeing only one second coming (*parousia*) of Christ to rapture the church and begin His wrath. My challenge is for everyone to carefully read the three "Second Coming" [*parousia*] passages of Matthew 24; 1 Thessalonians 4:13-18; and 2 Thessalonians 1:6-2:8 and see which interpretation is most natural and which appears to be forced. Is the Second Coming one event? Or are there two events or aspects of the Second Coming separated by seven years?

ii Is the Bema Seat of Christ Only for Believers?

There is a different judgment for true believers separate from the Great White Throne. It is called the *bema seat* of Christ. It has nothing to do with God's wrath, since Jesus satisfied His wrath for them on the cross (Matt. 27:45-46, 2 Cor. 5:21). The *bema* is a positive judgment for eternal rewards for believers based on the degree of their good works during their earthly lives. (See Romans 14:10, 1 Corinthians 3:10-16, and 2 Corinthians 5:10.) This judgment is not related to either the Day of the Lord's wrath at the end of the tribulation, nor His eternal punishment for unbelievers in the lake of fire after the Great White Throne judgment.

iii Who Will Repopulate the Earth After the Day of the Lord's Wrath?

Perhaps the following question has popped into your mind: *If all the believers get raptured and all the unbelievers are eventually killed by God's judgments, which end Daniel's 70ᵗʰ Week at Armageddon, who is going to repopulate the earth in physical bodies in the millennial kingdom?* This is the same question I used to ask (and still do) when challenging the posttribulation position when I still held to the pretribulation rapture. This is a really good question that prevented me from becoming a posttribulationist for many years. Who would survive the Day of the Lord, enter Christ's earthly kingdom with physical bodies, and fulfill all the prophecies that premillennialists believe the Bible predicts? One valid answer is that there will be some *not yet believers* during the tribulation who miss the rapture because they do not yet believe in Jesus, but they refuse to follow the Antichrist and take the mark of the beast (Rev. 13:16-17, 14:9-11, 20:4). These people will include the 144,000 sealed Jews (Rev. 7:1-8) and those Gentiles who quickly leave Jerusalem or wherever else they may be in order to escape the persecution of the Antichrist (Matt. 24:15-22). This idea is reflected in the fleeing of the woman presented in Revelation 12:1-2, 4-6, 13-17 (emphasis mine):

> A great sign appeared in heaven: a woman clothed with the sun, with a crown of twelve stars on her head. She was pregnant and cried out in pain as she was about to give birth…The dragon stood in front of the woman who was about to give birth, so that it might devour her child the moment he was born. She gave birth to a son, a male child, who "will rule all the nations with an iron scepter." And her child was snatched up to God and to his throne. *The woman fled into the wilderness to a place prepared for her by God, where she might be taken care of for 1,260 days*…When the dragon saw that he had been hurled to the earth, he pursued the woman who had given birth to the

male child. The woman was given the two wings of a great eagle, so that *she might fly to the place prepared for her in the wilderness, where she would be taken care of for a time, times and half a time, out of the serpent's reach. Then from his mouth the serpent spewed water like a river, to overtake the woman and sweep her away with the torrent. But the earth helped the woman by opening its mouth and swallowing the river that the dragon had spewed out of his mouth....* Then the dragon was enraged at the woman and went off to wage war against the rest of her offspring—those who keep God's commands and hold fast their testimony about Jesus.

We know that there are Gentiles in this new group who are born-again after the rapture since the judgment of the sheep and the goats (Matt. 25:31-46) is a judgment of *all the nations* when Jesus is on His throne and establishing the beginning His millennial reign. Many are designated as sheep (believers). These will inherit (take possession of) a portion of His kingdom as the reward for their faithfulness during the testing they endured through during Daniel's 70th Week, which they survived (Matthew 24:13, 22). They have not yet received their eternal glorified bodies, so they are still in their fleshly bodies. This means they will be able to enter into, reproduce, and repopulate the world during the millennial kingdom.

iv Aorist Tense Meanings

1) Pretribulation rapture teachers interpret the aorist tense to mean action that began in the past (in this case, beginning with the first seal) and continues for a period of time. This *constative* meaning is pointed out by the following Greek grammar textbooks:

> *The constative aorist*: The use of the aorist contemplates the action in its entirety. It takes an occurrence regardless of its extent of duration, gathers it into a single whole. "This temple was built (aorist) in forty-six years. [H. E. Dana and J.R. Mantey, *A Manual Grammar of the Greek New Testament* (Toronto: Macmillan, 1957), 196].

> *The constative*: the action is looked upon in its entirety. The act may have covered considerable time but is presented as one act. [Ray Summers, *Essentials of New Testament Greek* (Nashville: Broadman Press, 1950), 67].

2) Prewrath teachers believe that the aorist means action that is just beginning. This means the action is *in the future*. The same two Greek grammarians discuss this *ingressive* sense to describe the verbal action as about to begin:

> *Ingressive:* the beginning of the action is emphasized when a state or condition is being entered into. (Jesus is praying in the Garden of Gethsemane) "The hour *has come* (aorist), behold the

Son of Man is being betrayed into the hands of sinners." (Mark
14:41) Jesus says this when He knew the time of His arrest, trial,
and crucifixion are about to happen in the future. (*Essentials of
New Testament Greek* by Ray Summers, p. 67, and *A Manual
Grammar of The Greek New Testament,* by H. E. Dana and
Julius Mantey, 196.)

Another Greek scholar included the *futuristic* nuance of the aorist in his grammar
book:

It is a vivid transference of the action to the future. "If your
brother sins, go and reprove him in private, if he listens to you,
you *have won* (aorist) your brother." (Matt. 18:15, NASB)
[A.T. Robertson, *A Grammar of the Greek New Testament in
the Light of Historical Research* (Nashville: Broadman Press,
1934), 846].

Although the English might be translated such that we would understand it as past
action, there is a future result yet to come. Suitable translations could also be "you
will win your brother" or "you will have won your brother." Either way, the idea
is that the restoration of fellowship is a future result after the reproving and
listening. Still another Greek scholar recognizes the futuristic shade of meaning
for the aorist, labeling it as *proleptic:*

The aorist can have a phenomenally wide range of usage. You
can be looking at the action as a whole, but paying special
attention to the beginning, or to the end. It can describe
something that simply is, regardless of any time reference. But
my favorite is the proleptic (futuristic) use of the aorist. Because
time is secondary, the aorist can describe a future event and
emphasize the certainty of the action. (Bill Mounce, *The Aorist
Is So Much More Than a Past Tense*, from his blog *Monday
With Mounce*, billmounce.com, February 23, 2014)

The Berean Christian Bible Study Resources website link (*Greek
Grammar/Greek Tense/Aorist,* February 10. 2009) also discusses the proleptic
(futuristic) nuance and gives an example from Romans 8:30, which reads:

... and whom He predestined, these He also called, and whom
He called, these He also justified; and whom He justified, these
He also glorified [aorist].

Notice that, in every major English translation, the verb tense of God glorifying
people is aorist and translated in English as if it were already accomplished in
time past. However, most interpreters understand this glorifying of Christians to
be accomplished in the future. Theologian John Murray, as an example, sees the
aorist verb translated into an English past tense form, but the meaning is actually
a future act of God:

Glorification unlike calling and justification *belongs to the future*… though "glorified" is in the (English) past tense, this is proleptic, intimating the certainty of its accomplishment. (John Murray, *The NICNT Commentary: Epistle to the Romans* (Grand Rapids: Eerdmans Publishing, 1982 reprint), Volume I, 321.

To summarize, the aorist tense can have a variety of meanings concerning the action of the verb. One is *constative,* which sees the action as one whole event. Another, the *proleptic/ingressive* aorist, is when the action is in the future or just beginning. Sometimes, English translations makes the *proleptic/ingressive* appear to be past action, but because the emphasis is on the speaker's certainty that it will take place, it is translated it as if it has already been accomplished. The question we must try to answer about the aorist in Revelation 6:17 is "What are the people saying about the action of the arrival of God's wrath?" Is it just beginning? Is it just ending? Has it been going on? Is it over with? Or is it in the future? The aorist tense can allow for any of these. However, the context favors that it is about to begin.

ᵛ Addressing David Hocking's Sermon

I have a recording from a sermon given by Bible teacher and pastor David Hocking from the early 1980s in which he shares a conversation he had with a very wealthy and politically connected individual. The man told Mr. Hocking that he was the president of a small group of powerful people who have the goal of bringing about a one-world government, one-world economy, and one-world religion. He showed pictures of himself with these people to verify what he was saying. His particular emphasis was global economics, but he had just attended a meeting on bringing about one unified world religion. He explained that the group's motive was to bring about peace, since the primary things that cause divisions are people's disagreements over politics, economics, and religion. This group believed when those differences are eliminated, there would be world peace. According to Hocking, the man made two fascinating comments in the course of the conversation. First, the people of his group are highly secretive since they do not want others to know about what they are trying to do. Second, he said he was upset that there are certain people in the United States who are against what they are trying to do. Pastor Hocking was shocked by what he was hearing and notes the parallels between what this man was telling him and people during the future time of the Antichrist who desire peace, but the way they try to bring it about is to get rid of those who do not agree with them. Of course, this principle has been in action throughout history, and the extreme outworking of this principle has often been violence or war. It will be true in the future, too, just before the arrival of the Day of the Lord's wrath. Paul wrote that destruction will suddenly come upon those who are causing the tribulation under the Antichrist, who is attempting to bring them "peace and safety" (1 Thess. 5:3). To see the danger of this thinking, we only have to look back a few decades to the people of Germany and Japan to see what they did in their blindness by following after human leaders. Their Fuhrer and emperor promised them utopia on earth, with peace and prosperity. They only had to first get rid of those who disagreed with their philosophies. Fortunately, their goals were thwarted, just as the future Antichrist's will be because of the return of Jesus. Praise the Lord!

vi Dr. Garland on the Futuristic Aorist in Revelation 6:17, 11:15

In spite of seeing the aorist verb in Revelation 11:15 as futuristic, Dr. Garland rejects that nuance and the prewrath interpretation of the aorist in Revelation 6:17. Here are his comments on the aorist of *erchomai* (the Greek word which means "to come") in that verse:

> ἦλθεν [*elthen*], aorist tense which normally denotes past time. The day has already come in the opening of the sixth seal. God's wrath is being poured out prior to the seventh seal. This contradicts the pre-wrath rapture view which holds that the seals represent "Man's wrath through Antichrist". While it is true that the aorist tense can be used to describe a future event (proleptic), it is more often used of actions which have already transpired. Advocates of the pre-wrath rapture view argue that the pronouncement associated with the sixth seal is anticipatory of the wrath of God, and not in reaction to it. Since the aorist can represent events either in the past or future, the form of the verb itself (aorist) cannot settle the matter. Instead, the context must indicate which meaning is in view. The use of this same word within the larger context of the book of Revelation argues for understanding *has come* as denoting a past or present event which has just arrived.
> (www.spiritandtruth.org/teaching/Book_of_Revelation/comm entary/htm/chapters/06.html#3.6.17)

In this part of his commentary, Dr. Garland lists eleven occurrences of the aorist verb *elthen* in Revelation. All of the English translations translate both verses either "came" or "has come." Here is what he says about them:

> In each of these cases, the verb describes something in the past, in the present, or in the immediate future—having "just now" come... It is commonly used of a state which has just been realized, or a result which has just been accomplished, or is on the point of being accomplished. In none of its appearances in Revelation is it rendered by the translators as a true future tense (e.g., shall come, will come, is coming).

Dr. Garland acknowledges that in the eleven cases, it is possible for the aorist verb *elthen* to mean action that is in *the immediate future* and then defines that to mean *having just now come*. He mentions Revelation 14:7, "the hour of His judgment has come." He calls this *"a prophetic aorist, the time of His judgment is certain and imminent."* In his own words, he recognizes this is a futuristic aorist. Then, concerning Revelation 19:7, "the marriage of the Lamb has come," he states, "The time has arrived for Christ to marry His bride." Clearly, the marriage *will take place soon in the future.* Just as the marriage is about to occur in that verse, the wrath of God *is about to start* in Revelation 6:17. It has not been going on in the past, during the first five seals. In his earlier quotation, he twice acknowledged that the aorist can be futuristic. He says it can describe a future event, and it can be a state which is at the point of being accomplished.

However, as someone who holds the pretribulation rapture position, he attempts to shut out the futuristic meaning of the aorist here. He cites three reasons for doing so. First, he says it must be past action because that nuance is more common. However, scarcity of the futuristic nuance is no grounds for rejecting it. It is true that the majority of aorist verbs may not be futuristic, but disqualifying this interpretation cannot be done on these grounds, *especially since we saw many futuristic aorist meanings in Revelation* [see pp. 108-112] and the context fits nicely with a future nuance. Even Garland admits three out of the eleven uses of *ēlthen* in Revelation are ingressive or proleptic. The second reason he gives is that no English translations of these eleven passages have it as a *true future* tense. He gives examples by using "shall come," "will come," and "is coming" to explain what he means by a "true future." This leads to the following question, "What is the difference between these three English expressions that he claims are true futures, and an action that will take place in the immediate future?" Is one "more future" than the other? For example, let's say my birthday is tomorrow. Is it any "less future" than my summer vacation, which is six months away? They are both "truly future" from the perspective of the time about which they are being spoken, even though one is closer than the other. A third reason Dr. Garland rejects the future meanings of *ēlthen* is that he appears to be trusting the English translations rather than his own exegesis and the best contextual probability. In his commentary, *there is no detailed exegesis of all eleven occurrences of ēlthen* other than the one being discussed here, Revelation 6:17 which he attempts to use to discredit the prewrath rapture teaching.

Because of this, it is necessary to firmly challenge his statement quoted earlier: "It cannot possibly mean what prewrathers say it means because it doesn't fit with the larger context of Revelation." In spite of Dr. Garland's claim, a futuristic nuance "the wrath of God is coming," makes perfect sense in the context of Revelation 6:12-17.

vii 'Fallen' Babylon

This pattern of a mass evangelistic effort, which is then followed by God's future judgment, is also seen in the account of Noah when he built the ark before the flood (2 Pet. 2:5). This huge construction project took many decades, and during that time, the story would probably have circulated about a coming flood and the ark he is building would be a means to survive it. Unfortunately, there was no repentance, so complete destruction of everyone but Noah and his family followed. By contrast, in the preaching by Jonah to Nineveh, the people did repent, so no wrathful judgment ensued. In the Olivet Discourse, Jesus says that there will be a worldwide proclamation of the good news, followed by the end-of-the-age events. This will include His second coming and accompanying judgment (Matt 24:14, 29-41). Revelation 14:6 tells of worldwide preaching by an angel using the same aorist verb *ēlthen* as in Revelation 6:17. The judgment that follows in Revelation 14:7 reads, "the hour of His judgment has come." This aorist is translated as *past* action in English (NASB), but once again, it should better be translated as ingressive or futuristic, "the hour of His judgment *is about to come*."

Then a second angel announces in Revelation 14:8, "Fallen, fallen" (two aorist verbs), which are used in reference to Babylon, the great city. But this fall of Babylon is a prophecy about the future of the city for two reasons. First, the details of the destruction of Babylon are found later in Revelation 16:17-19:3. There, we are told the fall of the great city will take place at the seventh and final bowl judgment, which is future. Therefore, if the seventh bowl is future, and the fall of Babylon occurs at that time, then this event must be future also. Second, there are two future tense verbs in Revelation 14:10 describing the wrath that those who follow the beast will receive. The better translation of Revelation 14:8 is, "Babylon the Great will fall, will fall."

The same aorist verbal expression, "Fallen, fallen" is repeated in Revelation 18:2, and once again, we can know they have future nuances because of the announcement of the voice from heaven in Revelation 18:4. It is an encouragement for God's people to "come out of Babylon" because the fall *is coming soon*, in the future. The voice continues in Revelation 18:8-9, saying that Babylon's plagues *"will come"* (future tense) in a single day, and she *"shall be burned"* (future tense) and the kings *"will weep"* (future tense). Just one verse later, it says, "In one hour your judgment has come [the aorist verb *ēlthen*]." This must have future meaning as the angel is still prophesying about Babylon's coming plagues. All three aorist verbs make the most sense when understood to be something that is announced as if it has already happened (in the English translations), but the actual events themselves will occur in the future. The ingressive and future nuance of aorist verbs in Revelation concerning the future fall of Babylon give strong support for the same future meaning of the aorist concerning God's coming wrath in Revelation 6:17.

CHAPTER 9

CLOSING ARGUMENTS

To this point, we have looked at evidence that questions the pretribulation imminence teaching that the rapture could happen at any moment starting at the time of the apostles and that it is the next biblical prophecy to take place. Along with this, it was presented that the best interpretation is the prewrath teaching that the rapture *will become imminent* after the Antichrist is revealed halfway through Daniel's 70th Week, an event which is called the Abomination of Desolation.

One of my scholarly pretribulation rapture friends downplayed the significance of the amount of time difference between the two rapture teachings, saying, "It is not that important. The difference is only a few years." Unfortunately, this attitude is not uncommon among Christians in the United States. One must wonder if this mindset is because of the freedoms, prosperity, and security we are blessed to have. Most American Christians cannot imagine that any generation of the church could experience the final tribulation described in the Bible. In their minds, this could not possibly happen despite the fact that similar tribulation has occurred (and is still occurring) in many places around the world.

This mentality of indifference becomes even more deeply embedded when one's brain is locked in believing that the tribulation is one and the same with God's wrath and the church will not have to go through either of them. Anyone who has gone through persecution or suffering on account of their faith, or any sort of intense pain, even for just a short time, would likely argue that any amount of time is *too long*. The time of tribulation by any Christian should not be taken lightly, especially since the Bible tells those who believe in Christ are to expect tribulation:

> Remember the word that I said to you: "A slave is not greater than his master. If they persecuted Me, they will also persecute you; if they kept My word, they will keep yours also. But all these things they will do to you for My name's sake, because they do not know the One who sent Me." (John 15:20-21)

> Indeed, all who desire to live godly lives in Christ Jesus will be persecuted. (2 Tim. 3:12)

> After we had been there a number of days, a prophet named Agabus came down from Judea. Coming over to us, he took Paul's belt, tied his own feet and hands with it and said, "The Holy Spirit says: 'In this way the Jews of Jerusalem will bind the owner of this belt and hand him over to the Gentiles.'" When we heard this, we and the people there pleaded with Paul not to go up to Jerusalem. Then Paul answered, "Why are you weeping and breaking my heart? I am ready not only to be bound, but also to die in Jerusalem for the name of the Lord Jesus." (Acts 21:10-13, NIV)

All living disciples of Christ need to understand that the message of Jesus to His apostles in the Olivet Discourse, and also Paul's clear statements years later to the Thessalonians, are that *someday a generation of the church will face the Antichrist*. It was once said, "A person cannot really live for something, until they are ready to die for it." Today's church in America is presenting a good message that challenges all believers *to live for Jesus*, but is failing to prepare us to be willing *to die for Him*. The challenge to live a life of full surrender to Jesus is incomplete if the challenge to die for Jesus is not also included. In the United States, we often hear good messages about the difficulties in the Christian life, such as sickness, financial setbacks, or broken relationships. But when was the last time you heard a sermon on persecution or martyrdom? Are Bible teachers avoiding these topics because their messages do not fit in well with today's American pretribulation rapture culture that says, "We will be out of here before it gets too bad?" For most people that is a much more desirable teaching. It is little surprise that many have told me, "I believe the pretribulation view *because I want it to be true.*" But please note this, that our desires do not determine truth.

One's belief in the future greatly affects how they think and behave in the present. Could we, or any of our descendants, be among those who Jesus was referring to when He said:

> Then they will deliver you to tribulation, and will kill you, and you will be hated by all nations on account of My name. And at that time *many will fall away* and will deliver up one another and *hate one another.* And many false prophets will arise and will *mislead many.* And because lawlessness is increased, *most people's love will grow cold…* so, you too, when you see all these things, recognize that He is near, right at the door. Truly I say to you, this generation will not pass away until all these things take place. Heaven and earth will pass away, but My words shall not pass away. (Matt. 24:9-12; 33-34, emphasis added)

Remember, it was shown that Jesus was speaking to his disciples as believing Christians, not to the nation of Israel. He was making reference to whichever generation of His disciples who will be living and see the Antichrist and that horrible time of persecution taking place. If the church is programmed to believe that it will miss that terrible person and terrible time, but eventually finds itself there, it is understandable why Jesus predicted that many will fall away.

The Foundation of Imminence: Not What Many Think

The starting point of the trial was the statement of one of the pretribulation rapture position's own leading scholars who acknowledged that this view "is not explicitly taught" in the Bible. This admission should not be so surprising after we saw the weakness of the many proof texts used to teach that the rapture can happen at any moment. Close examination of all of those passages showed that their presupposition of present imminence is being read into every one of them. So, from the very get-go, the biblical foundation of the pretribulation teaching should be questioned.

The next point challenged was the claim that the apostles taught that the rapture has been the next Bible prophecy to be fulfilled from the time either of Christ's ascension or the sending of the Holy Spirit around AD 32. This was shown to be false in light of the prophecies made about Peter's death and Paul's trip to Jerusalem and Rome, all of which did not take place until approximately AD 65. Another prophecy disqualifying rapture imminence around that time was the destruction of Jerusalem and the Jewish temple, which was not fulfilled until AD 70. The historical fact of Israel's subsequent dispersion, after the pillaging of their capital city, made it impossible for Daniel's prophecy regarding the covenant between them and the Antichrist to be fulfilled under those circumstances. Pretribulation teachers say this will occur about the same time as their imminent rapture, but it could not have happened "at any moment" until Israel regained control of their Promised Land and capital city, Jerusalem. So, for 1900 years, the start of Daniel's 70th Week and the rapture could not have been imminent.

Some people will argue that the rapture has been imminent since Israel became a sovereign nation in 1948 or when they regained control of Jerusalem in 1967. Thus, an "any moment" rapture could have occurred at any time after that year. However, it was shown to be illogical for the prophesied events of the first three-and-one-half years of Daniel's 70th Week to unfold since that time up to today. The global atmosphere is headed toward a worldwide reception of the Antichrist, but it is not feasible for it to happen right now under the present world conditions.

More significantly, present rapture imminence was also shown to be disqualified by clear passages that say the presence of the Antichrist and the events of the tribulation must happen before Christ's coming and the Day of the Lord. Passages from Daniel, the Olivet Discourse, and the letters to the Thessalonians are in agreement that, once the Antichrist is revealed by his abomination of desolation proclamation, then Christ's return and the rapture will be imminent. This is exactly what the prewrath position says.

The important expression, the Day of the Lord, was studied in great detail, showing that *God's wrath is distinct from the tribulation.* This is critical in properly locating the time of the rapture. Contrary to the teachings of pretribulation scholars, the tribulation, which is described in the first five seals of Revelation 6, will engulf the world *before* the gathering/rapture of God's elect, which is His church. John's vision in Revelation shows that the Old Testament prophecy about the darkening of the universe, which Joel said would occur *before* the Day of the Lord and Jesus said would happen *after* the tribulation, is mentioned again by John as taking place at Jesus' glorious appearance at the sixth seal. At this same time, the unbelievers are attempting to hide while crying out that *God's wrath is about to arrive.* Further evidence for the rapture taking place at this time comes from the sudden appearance before God's throne of a great multitude of Christ worshippers who come *out of the great tribulation* according to Revelation 7:12-17 (see Appendix 1, page 137, for that discussion in detail). Immediately following this, the seventh seal's removal permits the scroll to be opened and God's angels to begin administering His age-ending wrath as described in the trumpets and the bowls.

This prewrath interpretation was shown to be consistent when applying good hermeneutical rules involving all the rapture passages, as well as sound logical reasoning related to past history and the present global conditions.

What Is Your Verdict?

If you are a pretribulation rapture believer, there is probably a variety of responses in your mind. Possibly you are attracted to it and accept the prewrath position because it clears up what may have been confusing to you previously. Perhaps you may be curious, but not convinced. Or you may be saying that this is a good attempt at challenging the teaching of the pretribulation rapture, but you wonder how prewrath could possibly be true when it is such a new teaching. "How could so many Bible teachers have missed it for so long?" This is not necessarily true because the early church fathers, the Christian scholars of the first centuries after Jesus and the apostles, clearly held to the belief that the church would face the Antichrist (see Appendix 4 on page 163 for details). The fact is that many difficult doctrines took decades, and sometimes centuries, of study and dialogue before the truth was uncovered.[48] Much debate has remained within Bible believing churches over many different theological issues. Unfortunately, this is one reason why we have so many Christian denominations and see churches split.

Wherever you are in this spectrum, your next objective could be to begin to get answers to your questions. Because I believed in the pretribulation rapture for 40 years, it took me some time to comprehend the prewrath view before I came to fully embrace it. The primary reason was that, initially, I had other priorities, and presently maybe you do too. The second reason was because, back then, there were not many resources for learning more. That is not the case now. Many authors, speakers, theologians, and ministries are explaining and defending this rapture view (see Appendix 7 on page 183 for other prewrath resources).

Some Challenging Conclusions for Bible Teachers

Whatever you do (or don't do), please do not say, "The rapture and eschatology are not that important." The instructions contained in the Olivet Discourse (Matt. 24:4, 6, 15-18, 20, 23, 26, 32, 42, 44; 25:13) are included in Christ's Great Commission "to teach everything He has commanded us, even to the end of this age" (Matt. 28:18-20). If you are one who believes it is okay to ignore or downplay eschatology, you have bought into a lie. Prophetic truth is a major theme running throughout the Bible, and indifference toward it would be disobedience. Any teacher of God's Word needs to be constantly reminded of their greater accountability before Him (James 3:1). This would include both what they teach and what they

---

[48] Just three examples of this are as follows: 1) What is the true nature of Jesus Christ? 2) The canon of the Bible: What books should be included or excluded? 3) What is the true teaching of salvation from hell? Many more could be listed.

avoid teaching. Remember:

> All Scripture is inspired by God and profitable for teaching, for reproof, for correction, for training in righteousness; so that the man of God may be adequate, equipped for every good work. (2 Tim. 3:16, 17)

This is not to suggest that one should read through Revelation this week and immediately begin a Bible study or sermon series on it. But pastors and teachers need to make sure they are making a good-conscience effort to study all of the different views with the help of the Holy Spirit. It takes a lot of time and work to be a good Bible teacher. That is why I do not take lightly what Paul also wrote to Timothy:

> Let the elders who rule well be considered worthy of double honor, especially those who work hard at preaching and teaching. (1 Tim. 5:17)

> Be diligent to present yourself approved to God as a workman who does not need to be ashamed, handling accurately the word of truth. (2 Tim. 2:15)

Finally, there is a sober warning given by John in Revelation concerning anyone who alters any of the prophecies recorded in it. I wonder how many of us know it is there?

> I testify to everyone who hears the words of the prophecy of this book: if anyone adds to them, God will add to him the plagues which are written in this book; and if anyone takes away from the words of the book of this prophecy, God will take away his part from the tree of life and from the holy city, which are written in this book. (Rev. 23:18-19)

Both the pretribulation and prewrath rapture positions claim the rapture is discussed in Revelation and both scholarly sides of the debate stake a claim as God's truth. However, they both cannot be true. One of my seminary professors, Dr. Norman Geisler, would often say: "If two of you disagree about something, then at least one of you is wrong." And of course there is also the possibility that both could be wrong. Our desire should be to have a spirit of humility and do our very best to not be wrong in anything we do in representing Christ, including teaching about His second coming. That is why I invite anyone to contact me if you think I have misrepresented God's Word and need correction. Note the invitation is not to contact me just because you disagree with me, I want to have meaningful exegetical dialogue about the text of the Bible. Along with this, let me know if you would like help in understanding the prewrath teaching. I am available to teach seminars on the rapture at no charge. Lastly, I am willing to have a friendly formal debate with any pretribulation rapture teacher about this issue of imminence which would help to educate those who come to it in being able to understand the issues involved with this great doctrine of Christ's return. God bless you, and thank you for persevering to the end (of this book). Remember…

Jesus is coming! Jesus is coming soon! Jesus is coming soon, but not as soon as you may think!

APPENDIX 1

THE RAPTURE IN THE BOOK OF REVELATION

Chapter 8 of this book offered a detailed discussion concerning the important questions of the *what* and *when* of God's future wrath on the earth. Pretribulationists claim God's end times vengeance begins with the first seal, so the rapture must take place just before this without any preliminary signs. They understand God's wrath to last all seven years of Daniel's 70th Week, and it consists of all of the seals, trumpets, and bowls. Prewrath sees God's wrath beginning once the seventh seal is removed, allowing for the trumpet and bowl judgments to be released through angels on the earth. The rapture takes place at the sixth seal, which means the first five seals are tribulation, but not God's wrath. Which interpretation has the best support for identifying the time of the rapture from the book of Revelation?

Locating the Prewrath Rapture in Revelation

The pretribulation believer might challenge the prewrath interpretation of the rapture by asking the following question:

> If the wrath of God was not present in the first five seals before Revelation 6:17, where is the rapture mentioned in the text if the judgments begin after the sixth?

This is a good question, but the same question also applies to the pretribulation rapture. Since the pretribulation rapture places the rapture before the opening of the first seal, where do they see the rapture in the text?

The prewrath response is found in the broader context surrounding Revelation 6:17. Prewrath locates the rapture in the events described by the sixth seal. Most students of prophecy agree that there is an interlude contained in Revelation 7, since the seventh seal is not removed until Revelation 8:1. Normally, we would expect the removal of the seventh seal to take place immediately after the sixth since this has been the pattern. The events of the first seal are described in Revelation 6:1-2; the second seal in 6:3-4; the third seal in 6:5-6; the fourth seal in 6:7-8; the fifth seal in 6:9-11; and the sixth seal in 6:12-17. But the breaking of the seventh seal does not occur until chapter eight. Why? We should be curious as to why there is a disruption in the pattern established with the first six seals.

That curiosity can be satisfied by examining three important subjects discussed in the Revelation 7:1-17. First, there is the *postponement* of God's wrath by the four angels (Rev. 7:1-3). Second, we see *protection* of 12,000 Jews from each of the 12 tribes of Israel (Rev. 7:4-8). Third, there is a *pullout* of the church (the rapture) before God's wrath when a great multitude of believers come out of the great tribulation (Rev. 7:9-17).

Let us examine these three points in greater detail.

1) God's *postponement* of His coming judgments:

> After this I saw four angels standing at the four corners of the earth, holding back the four winds of the earth, so that no wind would blow on the earth or on the sea or on any tree. And I saw another angel ascending from the rising of the sun, having the seal of the living God; and he cried out with a loud voice to the four angels to whom it was granted to harm the earth and the sea, saying, "Do not harm the earth or the sea or the trees until we have sealed the bond-servants of our God on their foreheads." (Rev. 7:1-3)

Here we see four angels "holding back the four winds of the earth." Whether this is referring to literal winds or is a figure of speech, the vision is communicating that God's angels are postponing destruction on the earth. This adds additional support to the fact that the earlier seals were not God's wrath, but that it occurs later, through the hands of His angels in the trumpets and the bowls. At this point, God's fury is being restrained to allow for the second and third events described in the rest of the Chapter 7 before His wrath begins in Chapter 8.

2) God's special seal of *protection*:

> And I heard the number of those who were sealed,
> one hundred and forty-four thousand sealed from all
> the tribes of the sons of Israel. (Rev. 7:4)

The second reason for the delay is a special task of a fifth angel, which is summarized in this verse. This event is of great significance. The correct interpretation seems to be straightforward in the context. This is a command from an authoritative angel for *the protection of a remnant of Jews from God's wrath that is about to come.* Remember the words of hope mentioned previously in the Old Testament (see Joel 3:16 and Zephaniah 2:3), where both prophets describe some who will escape the judgments of the Day of the Lord. The sealing of these Jews for protection is not the same as their becoming Christians. They will come to believe in Jesus later. These are physical descendants of Abraham who will refuse to follow the Antichrist during the tribulation. Since they are not believers at this time, they do not get raptured with the church. Rather, they have God's special protection, allowing them to survive the Day of the Lord. It is sometime during that period they will come to believe in Jesus as the true Messiah. These Jews are specifically singled out in this passage in order to fulfill the numerous eternal promises concerning physical seed of Abraham contained in the Abrahamic, Davidic, and New covenants. This is supported by Paul's teaching in Romans 9-11, where he states there will be a remnant of Israel that will be saved and later enter the millennial kingdom (see Romans 11:25-29). Since God cannot lie (Heb. 6:18), it makes sense that this sealing before the rapture is of a non-believing and non-raptured remnant group of Jews who will be protected as they live through God's wrath on the earth.

3) The great multitude *pulled out* during the great tribulation:

> After these things I looked, and behold, a great
> multitude which no one could count, from every nation
> and all tribes and peoples and tongues, standing before
> the throne and before the Lamb, clothed in white robes,
> and palm branches were in their hands; and they cry out
> with a loud voice, saying, "Salvation to our God who
> sits on the throne, and to the Lamb." (Rev. 7:9-10)

This is truly an extraordinary vision. Notice the expression "and
behold" in Revelation 7:9. This term expresses something to which
the speaker or writer is attempting to draw attention because of the
surprise or magnitude of what is being discussed. The text indicates
there is a great multitude from all nations, tribes, peoples, and
languages who have not been previously mentioned in the visions of
God's throne. The best understanding is that this new group of
worshippers is a gathering of believers who have just arrived in
heaven after being raptured out from the terrible time of the great
tribulation on earth. There are two good reasons for this.

First is because of what is said earlier in the sixth seal, *when Christ
appears*. The passage describes how the unbelievers are trembling
in fear because they face the one whom they have been persecuting
and who is now returning from heaven and about to pour out His
wrath: (also see p. 107-118 for more details)

> And the sky was split apart like a scroll when it is
> rolled up… And they said to the mountains and to the
> rocks, "Fall on us and hide us from the presence of
> Him who sits on the throne, and from the wrath of
> the Lamb; for the great day of their wrath has come,
> and who is able to stand?" (Rev. 6:14-17)

We also know from other Scriptures that the visible appearance of
Jesus in the sky brings not only God's impending wrath, but also
escape by rapture of the righteous (1 John 3:2, Titus 2:13, 1 Thess.
4:16-17, 2 Thess.1:6-8).

The second reason, and even more obvious, is John's conversation
with one of the elders concerning the identity of this large group that
the apostle does not recognize: (emphasis added)

> Then one of the elders asked me, "These in white robes—who are they, and where did they come from?" I answered, "Sir, you know." And he said, "These are they *who have come out of the great tribulation*; they have washed their robes and made them white in the blood of the Lamb." (Rev. 7:13-14 NIV)

Allowing Scripture to interpret Scripture, it makes the most sense that this huge multi-national, multi-ethnic, and multicultural group of people who come out of the great tribulation is the *raptured church*! The appearance of Jesus brings an end to the terrible affliction His followers have been experiencing under the Antichrist's persecution and begins God's punishment of the unbelievers who are followers of the man of sin:

> For then there will be great distress, unequaled from the beginning of the world until now—and never to be equaled again. If those days had not been cut short, no one would survive, but for the sake of the elect those days will be shortened. (Matt. 24:21-22, NIV)

> After all, it is only right for God to repay with affliction those who afflict you, and to grant relief to you who are oppressed and to us as well, when the Lord Jesus is revealed from heaven with His mighty angels in blazing fire. He will inflict vengeance on those who do not know God and do not obey the gospel of our Lord Jesus. (2 Thess. 1:6-8)

> For the Lord Himself will descend from heaven with a shout, with the voice of the archangel and with the trumpet of God, and the dead in Christ will rise first. Then we who are alive and remain will be caught up together with them in the clouds to meet the Lord in the air, and we shall always be with the Lord. (1 Thess. 4:16-17)

It is easy to recognize the similarity of these passages with the teaching of Jesus in His Olivet Discourse:

> But immediately *after* the tribulation of those days
> the sun will be darkened and the moon will not give
> its light, and the stars will fall from the sky, and the
> powers of the heavens will be shaken. And then the
> sign of the Son of Man *will appear in the sky*, and
> then all the tribes of the earth will mourn, and they
> will see the Son of Man *coming on the clouds of the
> sky with power and great glory*. And He will send
> forth His angels with a great trumpet and they will
> *gather together His elect* from the four winds, from
> one end of the sky to the other. (Matt. 24:29-31,
> emphasis added)

This matches up with the multitude in Revelation 7:9. There are so
many people in this group that they cannot be counted. They are
from every nation, tribe, and tongue; plus, they were not previously
mentioned as being in heaven alongside the 24 elders, four creatures,
and angels (Rev. 5:11). Lastly, they appear to have bodies, since
they are worshipping with palms in their hands. In spite of this,
pretribulation teachers contend that these "tribulation saints" are not
members of the raptured church, but rather individuals who come to
believe in Christ as a result of a great revival during the tribulation:

> The 144,000 Jews are a sort of "first fruit" of a
> redeemed Israel, and their mission seems to be to
> evangelize the post-rapture world and proclaim the
> gospel during the tribulation period. As a result of
> their ministry, millions, "a great multitude that no
> one could count, from every nation, tribe, people and
> language" will come to faith in Christ.[49]

The problem with this interpretation is that nowhere in Revelation
does it say the 144,000 Jews evangelize the world (see p. 156 for
more details). Nor is there any indication of a worldwide revival,
bringing salvation to multitudes during the tribulation.
Pretribulation rapture teachers read this salvation explosion into the
text because they must have some explanation for the great
multitude of worshippers of Jesus who appear in heaven between

---

[49] https://www.gotquestions.org/144000.html, January 9, 2019.

the sixth and seventh seals.

There are two more hurdles for the pretribulation rapture teaching regarding this mega-crowd of worshippers. First, how can these "tribulation saints," who would have been martyred over the course of those few years, *suddenly appear together as one large group*? It seems that instead there would be a steady stream of saints arriving in heaven as they are being killed. The prewrath rapture concurs with John's vision without difficulty since, via the rapture, the church suddenly arrives together. A second issue with the pretribulation view is, when do these supposed tribulation martyrs acquire their glorified bodies? Most pretribulation rapture teachers equate this multitude with the martyrs of the fifth seal (Rev. 6:9-11). This is encapsulated by the following comment by Dr. Walvoord: "The 'great multitude' represents an important portion of those mentioned in 6:9-11."[50]

This is easy to say, but it makes no sense in light of the clear differences between the two groups. The fifth seal people (Rev. 6:9-11) consist of only "souls under the altar" whose activity is pleading to God that He would avenge their deaths. By contrast, the great multitude is "standing before God's throne," praising God in glorified bodies (Rev. 7:9-10). Finally, and most significantly, if John had already seen this multitude at the fifth seal and had been aware of who they were, why would he indicate his ignorance of their identity (Rev. 7:13-14)? These cannot be the same tribulation saints of the fifth seal. Something very important must have taken place between these two scenes for which the pretribulation teaching cannot account, but prewrath does. The smaller group of martyred souls waiting under the altar during the fifth seal must be given resurrected and glorified bodies at some point. That point will occur after the fifth seal and simultaneously with the rest of the dead saints from past history. This combined assembly of resurrected saints will join the living saints who have survived the Antichrist's persecution and whose physical bodies will be transformed into their eternal glorified ones. Both of these groups of believers, resurrected and

---

[50] John F. Walvoord, *The Revelation of Jesus Christ* (Chicago: Moody, 18th printing, 1981), 146.

transformed, will meet Jesus in the air and go immediately into God's heavenly presence. Together they combine to make up the great multitude. *This is the location of the rapture in John's vision!* It occurs *after* the tribulation (the first five seals) and *before* God's wrath (the trumpets and the bowls).

John's vision of the sixth seal followed by the interlude of chapter seven give us details about the rapture without any contradiction of the following New Testament rapture passages:

1) There is a promise by Jesus to *return* for His followers:

> Let not your heart be troubled; believe in God, believe also in Me. In My Father's house are many dwelling places; if it were not so, I would have told you; for I go to prepare a place for you. And if I go and prepare a place for you, *I will come again* and receive you to Myself, that where I am, there you may be also. (John 14:1-3, emphasis added)

2) There is a promise of *resurrection* for dead saints and *transformation* of the living ones:

> Behold, I tell you a mystery; we will not all sleep, but *we will all be changed*, in a moment, in the twinkling of an eye, at the last trumpet; for the trumpet will sound, and the dead will be *raised imperishable*, and we will be *changed*. For this perishable must *put on the imperishable*, and this mortal must put on immortality. But when this perishable will have *put on the imperishable*, and this mortal will have *put on immortality*, then will come about the saying that is written, "Death is swallowed up in victory." (1 Cor. 15:51-54, emphasis added)

> (Note: the last trumpet is different from the seventh trumpet judgment of John's vision in Revelation.)

3) There is a promise of the *reunion* of living and dead disciples with Jesus at the rapture:

> But we do not want you to be uninformed, brethren, about those who are asleep, so that you will not

grieve as do the rest who have no hope. For if we believe that Jesus died and rose again, even so God will bring with Him those who have fallen asleep in Jesus. For this we say to you by the word of the Lord, that we who are alive and remain until the coming of the Lord, will not precede those who have fallen asleep. For the Lord Himself will descend from heaven with a shout, with the voice of the archangel and with the trumpet of God, and the dead in Christ will rise first. Then we who are alive and remain *will be caught up together* with them in the clouds to meet the Lord in the air, and so we shall always be with the Lord. (1 Thess. 4:13-18, emphasis added)

To summarize, the location of the prewrath rapture at the sixth seal is in harmony with all the passages associated with the rapture. The context of the sixth seal includes the often-repeated sign of cosmic disturbances, the darkening of the sun, moon, and stars. These are said by Jesus to occur *after the tribulation* and by Joel to be *before the Day of the Lord.* The return of Jesus at that time causes fear in unbelievers as they see the glorified Christ in the clouds and recognize that God's wrath will soon come upon them. That appearance is where the rapture happens, just as 1 Thessalonians 4:16-17 concurs. So while we do not see the rapture itself in Revelation, we do see the result of Christ's second coming: fear and trepidation from unbelievers, followed by the result of the rapture: the great multitude of worshippers who suddenly appear in heaven "having come out of the great tribulation." From a prewrath perspective, the rapture occurs after the first five seals of tribulation and just before the angels begin to administer the trumpets and bowls of God's wrath.

Locating the Pretribulation Rapture in Revelation

If the pretribulation rapture believer can question the location of a prewrath rapture in Revelation, it is only fair that the same question be asked of the pretribulation rapture: "Where is a pretribulation rapture found in Revelation *before the first seal*?" Recall that it has been admitted that there are no explicit passages that teach the pretribulation rapture, but most pretribulationists will appeal to two possible explanations to defend their position.

#1 The Missing Word "Church"

First, many proclaim that the word "church" *(ekklesia* in Greek) is not found in Revelation from 3:22 through 22:16. Therefore, the church is understood to be absent from the earth during the period of time of the seals, trumpets, and bowls.

> The church, as such, is never mentioned in any passage dealing with the tribulation... From the viewpoint of pure exposition, it is impossible for anyone to turn to a Tribulation passage and to show that the church is there. — Arnold G. Fruchtenbaum[51]

The logic is that since the word "church" is not mentioned in that extended part of John's vision, the rapture must have already occurred. This reasoning is very problematic.

First, the references to "church" in Revelation 2 and 3 have to do with local geographic groups of believers. In no place is there a reference to the *universal church*, which is the complete body of believers which will be raptured. The plural word "churches" is found eight times, but is focused on only the seven churches of that region in Asia Minor about which John was writing. The purpose of the use of "church" in those two chapters is to give specific exhortations to those local gatherings of Christians regarding their spiritual conditions during the first century. To conclude that the absence of the word after chapter three means the rapture of the universal church took place is a real stretch.

Next, it should be pointed out that the word "church" is found only sporadically in all of the books of the New Testament anyway, and in many of them, not at all. It is not found in the gospels of Mark, Luke, John; the epistles of 1 and 2 Peter, 1 and 2 John, or Jude. But that hardly means that the messages of those writings are not applicable to the Christians who were living in the areas to which the books were distributed. Along these same lines, former

---

[51] Arnold G. Fruchtenbaum, *The Footsteps of the Messiah* (San Antonio: Ariel Ministries, revised edition 2003), 151.

pretribulationist and now prewrath teacher Alan Kurschner says:

> The word "church" is absent from the rapture
> passages: 1 Thessalonians 4:13-17 and John 14:1-4.
> Following the pretribulationist's logic, are we right
> to conclude that the church will not be raptured? Of
> course not! [52]

Third, instead of the word "church" in Revelation 3:22 to 22:16,
John uses other words to identify Christians who will be living
during this time: "saints" (5:8; 8:3-4; 11:18; 13:7-10; 14:12; 16:6;
17:6; 18:20,24; 19:8; 20:9); "brethren" (6:11; 12:10; 19:10; 22:9);
"bondservants" (11:18; 19:2,5; 22:3,6); and "overcomers"
(victorious Christians in the churches in 2:11, 17, 26; 3:5, 12, 21).
Later, there are references to the activities of and the rewards
promised to overcomers in Rev. 12:11 and Rev. 21:7.

Look at the terms used in these passages describing these activities:

1. "Praise to God" in Revelation 5:9-10 used by those who were
purchased for God by His blood from every tribe and tongue and
people and nation who have been "made a kingdom and priests to
God" and who will reign upon the earth. That sure sounds like a
description of members of the church.

2. The spiritual battle going on in Revelation 12:10-17 includes
brethren; ones who overcame him by the blood of the Lamb and of
the word of their testimony; and the rest of the woman's offspring,
who keep the commandments of God and hold the testimony of
Jesus. Who else could these be other than the true church?

Fourth, Charles Cooper points out another problem for this position
(emphasis added):

> The fact that the term "church" does not appear in
> Revelation after chapter 4 is a very important
> question. The church does not show up on earth and
> *neither does it show up in heaven.* The fact that it

---

[52] Dr. Alan Kurschner, *"The Word "Church" in the Book of Revelation,"* post
from Eschatos Ministries website, December 15, 2011,
https://www.alankurschner.com/2011/12/15/why-is-the-word-church-not-
mentioned-in-revelation-4–21/

does not show up in heaven is an even greater problem for pretribulationists.[53]

At first, pretribulationists' appeal concerning the absence of the word "church" appears to be a good one, but it turns out to be an artificial argument attempting to keep the church out of the tribulation and support their belief in an "any moment" imminent rapture.

#2 The Rapture Is in Revelation 4:1-4

Two more arguments held by pretribulation rapture teachers come from John's vision which contains two symbols of the raptured church in heaven before the events of the seals. The passage states:

> After these things I looked and behold a door standing open in heaven, and the first voice which I had heard, like the sound of a trumpet speaking with me said, "*Come up here*, and I will show you what must take place after these things." Immediately I was *in the spirit*, and behold, a throne was standing in heaven, and One sitting on the throne. And He who was sitting was like a jasper stone and a sardius in appearance; and there was a rainbow around the throne, like an emerald in appearance. And around the throne were twenty-four thrones, and upon the thrones I saw *twenty-four elders sitting, clothed in white garments, and golden crowns on their heads*. (Rev. 4:1-4, emphasis added)

The first claim for seeing a rapture in this passage is John's change from physically being in his place of imprisonment on the island of Patmos to being "in the Spirit" in heaven (Rev. 4:1-2). Some teachers say this is a picture of the rapture. The second is the presence of the 24 elders before the throne of God (Rev. 4:4), whom they claim symbolize the raptured church in its glorified and righteous state, who will be rewarded and prepared to co-reign with Jesus in His millennial kingdom. These quotes from two familiar

---

[53] Charles Cooper, *Website: Sola Scriptura Presents*, article *A Response to Ron Graff*, www.solagroup.org/articles/endtimes/et_0010.html)

teachers of the pretribulation rapture sum up this argument:

> The open door and the voice which calls "come up
> hither" and John's presence in glory in the spirit,
> clearly indicate symbolically the fulfillment of 1
> Thessalonians 4:15-17. That for which the faithful
> remnant waited, the blessed hope of the Church, has
> suddenly come to pass. The departure of the true
> Church from the earth will be as sudden as its
> beginning (Acts 2:1-2). —A.C. Gaebelein[54]

> It seems to me best to see this as twenty-four elders
> representing a coronated, exalted, raptured church.
> —Dr. John MacArthur[55]

However, these pretribulation teachers have this interpretation
contradicted by their own colleagues who do not see John's
transport into heaven and the vision of the elders this way. The
following pretribulation teachers reject the idea of John's transport
into heaven "in the Spirit" as the rapture (emphasis added):

> There is *no convincing reason* why the seer's (John)
> being "in the Spirit" and being called into heaven
> typifies the rapture of the church any more than his
> being taken into the wilderness to view Babylon
> indicates that the church is there in exile. The phrase
> relates to the experience of the seer, and *not
> necessarily to that of the church.* — Merrill C.
> Tenney[56]

> Identification of the twenty-four elders *should not be
> dogmatically held,* but such evidence as there is
> seems to point to the conclusion that they may
> represent the church...Probably most New

---

[54] A.C. Gaebelein, *Gaebelein's Annotated Bible* (London: Forgotten Books,
2012), comments on Revelation 4:1.

[55] Dr. John MacArthur, *"A Trip to Heaven, Part 2,"* sermon, May 3, 1992
(www.gty.org., December 28, 2018)

[56] Merrill C. Tenney, *Interpreting Revelation* (Grand Rapids: Erdman's
Publishing, 1988), 141.

Testament scholars today interpret the elders as angels. — John F. Walvoord[57]

In short, the mention of the twenty-four elders in the book of Revelation *does not prove the pretribulational rapture.* — Keith H. Essex[58]

Among pretribulation rapture scholars, the arguments for seeing placement of their imminent rapture in Revelation are admittedly weak, even by some of their own. This being the case, it is speculative for pretribulationists to claim that the rapture will occur before the seals and the time of the great tribulation based on this passage.

More helpful details related to the identity of the elders can be found in the writings of the following authors, all of whom reject the elders being the church[59].

1. Steven Sherma, *"Who Are the 24 Elders?"*

2. Scott Pruitt, *"Who Are the 24 Elders in Revelation 5:6-10"*

3. Alan Kurschner, *"Revelation 5:9-10, 1st Person or 3rd Person?"*

4. Sola Scriptura, *Revelation Commentary*

Summary of the Rapture in Revelation

Pretribulation rapture teachers use the absence of the word "church" in chapters 4-22 to show why the church will be absent from the tribulation. John's experience of being caught up in the Spirit, and

---

57 John F. Walvoord, *The Revelation of Jesus Christ* (Moody Press, 18th Printing, 1981), 107, 118

58 Keith H. Essex, *"The Rapture and the Book of Revelation,"* The Master's Seminary Journal, 13/2, Fall 2002, 229

59 Steven Sherma, www.armageddonbooks.com/sherman2.html, 1/4/2019; Scott Pruitt, NoPretrib.com, 1/4/2019; Alan Kurschner, https://www.aomin.org/aoblog/2007/06/16/revelation-59-10-1st-person-us-or-3rd-person-them/; RevelationCommentary.org, Sola Scriptura,7/11/03; Chapter Four; comments on Revelation 4:4, http://www.revelationcommentary.org/04_chapter.html

the presence of the 24 elders in heaven as representing the raptured church in 4:1-4, are used as support for the rapture occurring before the seals. These views are rejected by even some of their own scholars indicating very weak support for their view of rapture imminence since they cannot agree that they are valid.

The prewrath position unanimously locates the rapture in Revelation after the first five seals, at some unknown time during the last half of Daniel's 70th Week, after the Antichrist is revealed. At the sixth seal, the supernatural darkening of the sun, moon, and stars will be followed by the glorious appearance of Jesus. We know from other passages that the rapture of His followers takes place at this time (Matthew 24:29-31; 1 Thess. 4:15-17; 2 Thess. 1:7; 1 John 3:2). In Revelation, we are given supplementary information to these passages related to what happens at the time of the rapture. We learn that the unbelievers will attempt to hide from God's soon-to-come wrath (Rev. 6:12-17), while heaven sees the sudden arrival of an international multitude of joyful worshippers who came from out of the great tribulation (Rev. 7:9-17). The long awaited and completed salvation promised to the followers of the Messiah has finally arrived (emphasis added):

> According to His great mercy He has caused us to be born again to a living hope through the resurrection of Jesus Christ from the dead, to obtain an inheritance that is imperishable and undefiled and will not fade away, reserved in heaven for you, who are protected by God's power through faith for *a salvation ready to be revealed in the last time.* In this you greatly rejoice, even though now for a little while, if necessary, you have been distressed by various trials, that the proof of your faith, being more precious than gold, which is perishable, even though tested by fire, may be found to result in praise and glory and honor *at the revelation of Jesus Christ*; and though you have not seen Him, you love Him; and though you do not see Him now, but believe in Him, you greatly rejoice with joy inexpressible and full of glory, *obtaining as the outcome of your faith, the salvation of your souls.* (1 Peter 1:3-9)

APPENDIX 2

THE RESTRAINER IN 2 THESALONIANS 2:5-12

Another subject of debate related to the timing of the rapture concerns the identification of "the restrainer."

> And you know *what restrains* him now, so that in his time he may be revealed. For the mystery of lawlessness is already at work; only he *who restrains* will do so until he is taken out of the way. And then that lawless one will be revealed whom the Lord will slay with the breath of His mouth and bring to an end by the appearance of His coming; that is, the one whose coming is in accord with the activity of Satan, with all power and signs and false wonders, and with all the deception of wickedness for those who perish, because they did not receive the love of the truth so as to be saved. And for this reason, God will send upon them a deluding influence so that they might believe what is false, in order that they all may be judged who did not believe the truth, but took pleasure in wickedness. (2 Thessalonians 2:5-12, emphasis added)

The debate concerns the identity of the restrainer of the lawless one. The passage indicates that at the time Paul wrote the letter, something was hindering the Antichrist from being manifested. This passage can also be translated "something [or someone] that restrains." All the major rapture positions agree that the restraint is presently in effect since we have not yet seen the eschatological Antichrist. However, once the restraint is removed, the conditions then will be such that the Antichrist will be revealed and have the freedom to do what Satan desires him to do. At that time, the biblical prophecies about the destruction he will bring upon the world will come to pass.

There are many possibilities suggested as to the identity of the restrainer, including God the Father, God the Holy Spirit, the universal church, human government, the Roman Empire, and the preaching of the gospel by the church to name a few. The most popular view among pretribulationists holds that the restrainer is the Holy Spirit, in some capacity, usually by saying it is the influence of the Holy Spirit in the presence of the church on earth:

> The indication here is that as long as the Holy Spirit
> is resident within the church, which is His temple,
> this restraining work will continue and the man of sin
> cannot be revealed. It is only when the church, the
> temple, is removed that this restraining ministry
> ceases and lawlessness can produce the lawless one.
> — Dr. J. Dwight Pentecost[60]

Those who agree with this view contend that once the church is raptured, it takes with it this restraining power of God's Spirit. Satan will then be able to have his greatest control of the world ever through the beast and the false prophet. They say the pretribulation rapture cannot happen after the Antichrist is revealed, since his presence would be an observable prophecy before the rapture and ruin their view of imminence. So, most pretribulationists accept this interpretation of the restrainer being the church in spite of the following theological problems:

1. In the context of 2 Thessalonians 2, some pretribulationists go back to verse three and claim that *the apostasy*, which Paul says must come before the Day of the Lord, is the rapture because they think the word here means the physical departure of the church from the earth. This interpretation supports the idea that the restrainer must be the church prior

---

[60] Dr. J. Dwight Pentecost, *Things to Come*, 205.

to a pretribulation rapture. This position does not hold up because the Greek word for "apostasy" (apostasia) never refers to a physical or spatial departure or separation of one object from another. Rather, it refers to a political or religious falling away from a conviction that was previously held. Please see the following article for the more technical details: "Does 2 Thessalonians 2:3 Mention the Rapture?"[61]

2. Looking at Scriptures and church history, it should be obvious that the church has not been successful in restraining the many "antichrists" (with little "a"), even though God's Word commands it to do so. God has given the church His indwelling Holy Spirit in order to help Christians individually and collectively to accomplish that task. We only have to look at how, for thea most part of two thousand years, the church has been ineffective in resisting the schemes that Satan has used through his many antichrists to thwart God's will, especially the Great Commission. Therefore, it is doubtful that the universal church could have been, either in the past or present, the restraining force of the Antichrist (capital "A"). There are many verses about antichrists in 1 John 2:18-22; 4:1-6; and 2 John 7, and it is possible that individual believers can resist their false teachings and live apart from their influence. But the claim that the church is the restrainer of the eschatological Antichrist is a forced conclusion.

3. Along with this same idea, pretribulationists believe that the great multitude that appears in heaven worshipping at God's throne in Revelation 7:9-17 is comprised of those converted to Christ during the tribulation in a global revival after the rapture. They are then persecuted and martyred at the hand of the Antichrist. There is a major problem with this. If pretribulationists claim that the church had been restraining the Antichrist's ability to come into the world before the rapture, it does not make sense that after this restraining church is removed, a new group of tribulation converts

---

[61] https://www.alankurschner.com/2015/09/11/does-apostasia-in-2-thessalonians-23-refer-to-a-physical-departure-i-e-the-rapture/.

(pretribber's great multitude) who are committed and strong enough in their faith to die for Jesus are not able to restrain the Antichrist during that time too. Especially since we know about just two witnesses for Christ who will be able to stand against the Antichrist for 42 months until they are martyred (Rev. 11:3-12). The church is not the restrainer hindering the arrival of the Antichrist, but rather is a part of the group of saints who are resurrected and raptured during the time of the Antichrist great tribulation, cutting it short and ushering in God's wrath. .

4. Another pretribulation difficulty exists. Who will accomplish the missionary task of converting the great multitude during the tribulation if all the members of the restraining church are no longer on earth? Who will do the preaching to such a great number of people so they can be saved? The usual pretrib response is that the 144,000 sealed Jews will convert to Jesus during the tribulation and complete this evangelistic thrust. The problem is that nowhere does it say the 144,000 become Jewish evangelists. They do become followers of Christ according to Revelation 14:1-5, but there is no mention of them doing worldwide evangelism. This is another idea that must be read into the text. The only mass evangelism mentioned in the Bible being done at that time is by the two witnesses in Revelation 11 and also by an angel:

> I saw another angel flying in midheaven, having an eternal gospel to preach to those who live on the earth, and to every nation and tribe and tongue and people; and he said with a loud voice, "Fear God, and give Him glory, because the hour of His judgment has come."
> (Rev. 14:6-7)

This claim of a huge revival during the tribulation that converts a great multitude actually contradicts what Scripture indicates takes place in the lives of most of the people living during God's wrath. Revelation says that the more judgment people experience from God, the more they will harden their hearts against Him. There will undoubtedly be some who become believers during the Day of the Lord (recall Joel 3:16 and Zephaniah 2:3), but not a great multitude as pretribulationism contend. The prewrath understanding is that the great multitude is the collective group of saints of all time, dead and alive. They are the Old Testament and New Testament believers who will be resurrected or transformed together, then be raptured at the sixth seal's appearance of Jesus in the sky. This results in the cutting off the great tribulation and beginning of God's wrath when the seventh seal is removed from the scroll.

These four issues must be dealt with if one considers the restrainer to be the church before the pretribulation rapture. An alternative interpretation that avoids these tensions is that the restrainer is not the church at all, but Michael the Archangel. This means that the church will still be present on the earth during the great tribulation. Dr. Alan Kurschner summarizes some reasons for supporting this view based on research by Colin R. Nicholl:

> Recently there has been ground-breaking research on this topic by Thessalonian scholar Colin R. Nicholl. He contends that the *restrainer* Paul is referring to is Michael the Archangel. Here is an outline of his arguments:
>
> 1) In contemporary Jewish literature, the characteristics used to describe Michael establish him as having eschatological preeminence as the chief opponent of Satan and the restrainer of God's people.
>
> 2) Michael is viewed as a celestial restrainer of God's people in Daniel 10-12, the larger passage that serves as the source for Paul's explanation in 2 Thessalonians 2:3-8.
>
> 3) Daniel's use of the Hebrew word *md* in Daniel 12:1 comports with the ceasing activity of the restrainer in 2 Thessalonians 2:6-7.
>
> 4) The Greek term *parerchomai* in Daniel 12:1 of the Septuagint (LXX) means "to pass by," which shows that the ancient Jewish interpretation of this text

viewed Michael ceasing his restraint at this
eschatological event. Instructing on the restrainer in
2 Thessalonians 2:6-7, Paul is most likely drawing
from Daniel's text.

5) Early Rabbinic interpretation of Daniel 12:1
conveyed Michael as "passing aside" or
"withdrawing" in relation to the Antichrist's
establishment near or at the Temple Mount (Dan.
11:45) and just before the unequaled, eschatological
tribulation against God's people (Dan. 12:1).

6) Revelation 12:7-17 supports viewing Michael as
the restrainer because it links Michael's heavenly
war against the dragon with the eschatological
persecution of God's people (cf. 2 Thess. 2:6-7; Dan.
11:45-12:1).

These reasons strongly suggest that in 2
Thessalonians 2:6-7 the apostle sees Michael the
Archangel as the restrainer, whose ministry ceases
and causes the eschatological temple to be desolated
by the Antichrist, an event that is ensued by the
Antichrist's great tribulation against God's people.[62]

This explanation fits beautifully with the Scriptures in light of Paul's
previous statement about the Day of the Lord in 2 Thessalonians
2:3-4, which says it will not come unless the apostasy comes first
and the man of sin is revealed. God's wrath does not come
unannounced, since it is preceded by the presence of the Antichrist
and the hatred he takes out on the church and others who do not
follow him. The church has always been a restrainer of (and
influence against) sin on the earth and has had a ministry of
delivering people from demonic influence. However, these
ministries should not be confused with restraining the eschatological
arrival of the Antichrist.

---

[62] Dr. Alan Kurschner *Antichrist Before the Day of the Lord*, pp. 38-39.
Summarized from Colin R. Nicholl's article *"Michael, The Restrainer Removed
(2 Thessalonians 2:6-7)*, Journal of Theological Studies" 51 (2000): 27-53.

APPENDIX 3

IMMINENCE COMES AFTER THE ABOMINATION OF DESOLATION

As mentioned in Chapter 1, the prewrath position agrees with the pretribulation teaching that the rapture is an imminent event that will occur at some future unknown day. The difference between the two is that pretribulationists believe that imminence *is in effect right now* and has been for a long time. Prewrath contends that there are certain biblical prophecies that must occur first, and *then the rapture will become imminent.*

The prewrath interpretation states that some generation of Christians will enter Daniel's 70th Week, which will begin when Israel signs a covenant with a political leader who quickly acquires great international influence. His goal will be to bring world peace by means of economic, religious, and political unity under his control. According to John's visions in Revelation, this individual's efforts will be helped by an assistant, the false prophet, who does supernatural manifestations that encourage people to embrace this Antichrist and even take a mark that indicates their loyalty to him. Both Jews and Gentiles who have already become believers in Jesus, along with others who are not yet Christians, will begin to experience persecution because they refuse to take his mark. These things coincide with what Jesus discussed in the Olivet Discourse when He answered His disciples' questions about the future events:

> When will these things be, and what will be the sign
> of your coming and the end of the age? (Matt. 24:3).

Jesus tells them of many terrible events which His disciples will have to live through or for which they will have to die. The first part is referred to as "the beginning birth pangs" (Matt. 24:8). Later, the circumstances will get worse, a time Jesus labels as "tribulation," which eventually escalates into "great tribulation" (Matt. 24:9, 21). While Jesus is predicting these events, He singles out a specific event that stands out from the rest. This event has its origin with the Old Testament prophet Daniel:

> And he [the Antichrist] will make a firm covenant with the many [Israel] for one week, but in the middle of the week he will put a stop to sacrifice and grain offering; and on the wing of *abominations* will come one [the Antichrist] who makes *desolate*, even until a complete destruction, one that is decreed, is poured out on the one who makes desolate.... Many will be purged, purified and refined, but the wicked will act wickedly; and none of the wicked will understand, but those who have insight will understand. And from the time that the regular sacrifice is abolished and *the abomination of desolation* is set up, there will be 1,290 days. (Dan. 9:27; 12:10-11, emphasis added)

Most premillennial teachers, no matter which rapture position they hold, agree that Jesus is referencing this prophecy when he taught His disciples on Mount Olivet:

> "Therefore when you see *the abomination of desolation, which was spoken of through Daniel* the prophet, standing in the holy place (let the reader understand), then let those who are in Judea flee to the mountains; let him who is on the housetop not go down to get the things out that are in his house; and let him who is in the field not turn back to get his cloak. But woe to those who are with child and to those who nurse babes in those days! But pray that your flight may not be in the winter, or on a Sabbath; for *then there will be a great tribulation*, such as has not occurred since the beginning of the world until

now, nor ever shall. And unless those days had been
cut short, no life would have been saved; but for the
sake of the elect those days will be cut short." (Matt.
24:15-22, emphasis added)

Jesus uses Daniel's prophecy to identify this act of the Antichrist,
which will take place at the midpoint of Daniel's 70th Week, when
the Messianic imposter goes into the Jewish holy place and stops
their sacrifices and worship. In the highest form of blasphemy
against God, he goes so far as demanding to be worshipped as God.
This false Christ has the purpose of stealing for himself the glory
that is due only for the true Christ. There will be such a strong
temptation to follow the Antichrist that even true Christians will
have the potential to be deceived (Matt. 24:4-6, 10-11, 23-24).

In spite of previously telling the Thessalonians about these things
personally, Paul had to repeat this information in order to correct a
rumor that they were already in the Day of the Lord's wrath and may
have missed the rapture:

Concerning *the coming of our Lord Jesus Christ and
our being gathered to him,* we ask you, brothers, not
to become easily unsettled or alarmed by some
prophecy, report or letter supposed to have come
from us, saying that the Day of the Lord has already
come. Don't let anyone deceive you in any way, for
that day will not come until the rebellion occurs *and
the man of lawlessness is revealed, the man doomed
to destruction.* He will oppose and will exalt himself
over everything that is called God or is worshiped, so
that he sets himself up in God's temple, proclaiming
himself to be God. Don't you remember that when I
was with you, I used to tell you these things? (2
Thess. 2:1-5, NIV, emphasis added)

To paraphrase Paul's words, the church of true believers is being
told by both Jesus and Paul that some generation of them will go
through a horrendous time of testing and persecution. This is part of
God's sovereign plan and is necessary for God's purposes before He
brings this sinful age to an end. But *the days of this future tribulation
are not God's wrath* because the Day of the Lord cannot come

unless the man of lawlessness comes on the scene first and commits a very public and observable action—he goes into the temple and demands to be worshipped as God. That revelation of the Antichrist is the last prophecy required to be fulfilled before Jesus can make His appearance at some future unknown day or hour. It is at His supernatural second coming that He will resurrect and rapture His elect, bringing an end to the great tribulation, and begin to pour out His wrath against His enemies.

Notice that after Jesus shares these details in Matthew 24:3-31, He continues to give the disciples more information concerning their questions that would shape their minds about His return:

> "Now learn the parable from the fig tree: when its branch has already become tender, and puts forth its leaves, you will know the summer is near; even so you too, *when you see all these things*, recognize that He is near, right at the door." (Matt. 24:32-33, emphasis added)

In other words, when Christians will find themselves facing the Antichrist during the great tribulation, *they will know then* that the rapture is imminent. The last specific prophecy given by Jesus that needs to be fulfilled is the abomination of desolation in the holy place in Jerusalem. This summarizes the second goal of this book— to explain the truth about the imminence of the rapture. It cannot happen right now, but it will be imminent in the future.

APPENDIX 4

THE CHURCH FATHERS ON THE CHURCH AND THE TRIBULATION

I have read the arguments of some pretribulation rapture teachers who appeal to the early church father's writings to support their understanding of rapture imminence. However, the quotes they use are either simply appeals by the fathers to be ready to meet the Lord (expectancy) or they are taken out of the larger context and do not teach the church's absence on earth during the time of the Antichrist. Take, for example, the following statement by Dr. Dwight Pentecost: (emphasis added)

> Several citations may be made at this point to show that the early church held to the doctrine of imminency. Clement wrote in the *First Epistle to the Corinthians*: "Ye see how *in a little while* the fruit of the trees come to maturity. Of a truth, *soon and suddenly* shall His will be accomplished, as the Scriptures also bear witness, saying "*Speedily will He come, and will not tarry*"; and "The Lord *shall suddenly come* to His Temple, even the Holy One, for whom you look." In the *Didache* we read: "Watch for your life's sake. Let not your lamps be quenched, nor your loins unloosed; but be ye ready, *for ye know not the hour which our Lord cometh.*" ... These give evidence that the exhortation to watchfulness addressed to the church became the hope of the early church and that they lived in the light off the

expectation of the imminent return of Christ. The testimony of the Scripture and the evidence of the early church cannot be denied.[63]

With all due respect to my former professor, I believe it can be denied since it was shown in Chapter 2 how the Scriptures used to support the pretribulation understanding of rapture imminence are inaccurately interpreted. Similarly, I now contend that these statements of early church leaders, while they do exhibit *expectancy* and *anticipation* for Christ's second coming, contain nothing to clearly indicate that He will return at any moment or that the rapture was the next biblical prophecy to be fulfilled at the time they were writing. This is especially true since the church fathers wrote their material when the signing of a covenant between the Antichrist and Israel (prophesied in Daniel 9:27) was not just unreasonable, but impossible. Since AD 70, dispersed Israel was far from existing as a nation at the time they wrote. The following quotations contain emphasized phrases which clearly refute pretribulation rapture scholars' claims that the church will not have to face the Antichrist.

Quotations of Early Church Fathers in Their Full Context

A. From *Treatise on Christ and Antichrist* by Hippolytus (c.170- c. 235):

60. Now, concerning *the tribulation of the persecution which is to fall upon the church from the adversary*, John also speaks thus: "And I saw a great and wondrous sign in heaven; a woman clothed with the sun, and the moon under her feet, and upon her head a crown of twelve stars. And she, being with child, cries, travailing in birth, and pained to be delivered. And the dragon stood before the woman which was ready to be delivered, for to devour her child as soon as it was born. And she brought forth a man-child, who is to rule all the nations: and the child was caught up unto God and to His throne. And the woman fled into the wilderness, where she hath the place prepared of God, that they should feed her there a thousand two hundred and threescore days. And then when the dragon saw it, he persecuted the woman which brought forth the man-child. And

---

[63] Dr. J. Dwight Pentecost, *Things to Come*, 168-169.

to the woman were given two wings of the great eagle, that she might fly into the wilderness, where she is nourished for a time, and times, and half a time, from the face of the serpent. And the serpent cast (out of his mouth water as a flood after the woman, that he might cause her to be carried away of the flood. And the earth helped the woman, and opened her mouth, and swallowed up the flood which the dragon cast) out of his mouth. And the dragon was wroth with the woman and went to make war with the saints of her seed, which keep the commandments of God, and have the testimony of Jesus."

61. By "the woman then clothed with the sun," he meant most manifestly *the church,* endued with the Father's word, whose brightness is above the sun. And by the "moon under her feet" he referred to her being adorned, like the moon, with heavenly glory. And the words, "upon her head a crown of twelve stars," refer to the twelve apostles by whom the church was founded. And those, "she, being with child, cries, travailing in birth, and pained to be delivered," mean that the church will not cease to bear from her heart the Word that is persecuted by the unbelieving in the world. "And she brought forth," he says, "a man-child, who is to rule all the nations;" by which is meant that the church, always bringing forth Christ, the perfect man-child of God, who is declared to be God and man, becomes the instructor of all the nations. And the words, "her child was caught up unto God and to His throne," signify that he who is always born of her is a heavenly king, and not an earthly; even as David also declared of old when he said, "The Lord said unto my Lord, Sit Thou at my right hand, until I make Thine enemies Thy footstool." "And the dragon," he says, "saw and persecuted the woman which brought forth the man-child. And to the woman were given two wings of the great eagle, that she might fly into the wilderness, where she is nourished for a time, and times, and half a time, from the face of the serpent." *That refers to the one thousand two hundred and threescore days (the half of the week) during which the tyrant is to reign and persecute the church,* which flees from city to city, and seeks conceal-meat in the wilderness among the mountains, possessed of no other defence than the two wings of the great eagle, that is to say, the faith of Jesus Christ, who, in stretching forth His holy hands on the holy tree, unfolded two wings, the right and the left, and called to Him all who believed upon Him, and

covered them as a hen her chickens. For by the mouth of Malachi also He speaks thus: "And unto you that fear my name shall the Sun of righteousness arise with healing in His wings."

62. The Lord also says, *"When ye shall see the abomination of desolation* stand in the holy place (whoso readeth, let him understand), then let them which be in Judea flee into the mountains, and let him which is on the housetop not come down to take his clothes; neither let him which is in the field return back to take anything out of his house. And woe unto them that are with child, and to them that give suck, in those days! for then shall be great tribulation, such as was not since the beginning of the world. And except those days should be shortened, there should no flesh be saved." And Daniel says, "And they shall place the abomination of desolation a thousand two hundred and ninety days. Blessed is he that waiteth, and cometh to the thousand two hundred and ninety-five days."

63. And the blessed Apostle Paul, writing to the Thessalonians, says: "Now we beseech you, brethren, concerning the coming of our Lord Jesus Christ, and our gathering together at it, that ye be not soon shaken in mind, or be troubled, neither by spirit, nor by word, nor by letters as from us, as that the day of the Lord is at hand. Let no man deceive you by any means; for (that day shall not come) except there come the falling away first, and that man of sin be revealed, the son of perdition, who opposeth and exalteth himself above all that is called God, or that is worshipped: so that he sitteth in the temple of God, showing himself that he is God. Remember ye not, that when I was yet with you, I told you these things? And now ye know what withholdeth, that he might be revealed in his time. For the mystery of iniquity doth already work; only he who now letteth (will let), until he be taken out of the way. And then shall that wicked be revealed, whom the Lord Jesus shall consume with the Spirit of His mouth, and shall destroy with the brightness of His coming: (even him) whose coming is after the working of Satan, with all power, and signs, and lying wonders, and with all deceivableness of unrighteousness in them that perish; because they received not the love of the truth. And for this cause, God shall send them strong delusion, that they should believe a lie: that they all might be damned who believed not the truth, but had pleasure in

unrighteousness." And Esaias says, "Let the wicked be cut off, that he behold not the glory of the Lord."

64. *These things, then, being to come to pass, beloved,* and the one week being divided into two parts, and the abomination of desolation being manifested then, and the two prophets and forerunners of the Lord having finished their course, and the whole world finally approaching the consummation, *what remains but the coming of our Lord and Saviour Jesus Christ from heaven, for whom we have looked in hope*? who shall bring the conflagration and just judgment upon all who have refused to believe on Him.

B. Tertullian (c.155- c. 220): *On the Resurrection of the Flesh* (Chapters 25 and 41)

In the Revelation of John, again, the order of these times is spread out to view, which the souls of the martyrs are taught to wait for beneath the altar, while they earnestly pray to be avenged and judged: Revelation 6:9-10 (taught, I say, to wait), in order that the world may first drink to the dregs the plagues that await it out of the vials of the angels, Revelation xvi and that the city of fornication may receive from the ten kings its deserved doom, Revelation xviii and that the beast Antichrist with his false prophet may wage war on the church of God.

For the apostle makes a distinction, when he goes on to say, For in this we groan, earnestly desiring to be clothed upon with our house which is from heaven, if so be that being clothed we shall not be found naked; 2 Corinthians 5:2-3 which means, before we put off the garment of the flesh, we wish to be clothed with the celestial glory of immortality. Now the privilege of this favour awaits those who shall at the coming of the Lord be found in the flesh, and who shall, owing to the oppressions of the time of Antichrist, deserve by an instantaneous death, which is accomplished by a sudden change, to become qualified to join the rising saints; as he writes to the Thessalonians: For this we say unto you by the word of the Lord, that we which are alive and remain unto the coming of the Lord shall not prevent them which are asleep. For the Lord Himself shall descend from heaven with a shout, with the voice of the archangel, and with the trump of God: and the dead in Christ shall rise first: then we too shall ourselves be caught up together with them in the clouds, to meet the Lord in the air: and so shall we ever be with the Lord. 1 Thessalonians 4:15-17

C. Justin Martyr (c.100- c.165): *Dialogue With Trypho*

O unreasoning men! understanding not what has been proved by all these passages, that two advents of Christ have been announced: the one, in which He is set forth as suffering, inglorious, dishonored, and crucified; but the other, in which He shall come from heaven with glory, when *the man of apostasy, who speaks strange things against the Most High, shall venture to do unlawful deeds on the earth against us the Christians,*

D. *The Didache* (100- 120, the earliest Christian writings after the completion of the inspired New Testament writings):

Chapter 10. Remember, Lord, *Thy Church*, to deliver it from all evil and to make it perfect in Thy love, and *gather it from the four winds,* sanctified for Thy kingdom which Thou have prepared for it. [Note: Compare this to what Jesus said in Matthew 24:31: "And He shall send His angels with a great sound of a trumpet, and *they will gather together His elect from the four winds*, from one end of heaven to the other."]

Chapter 16. Watch for your life's sake. Let not your lamps be quenched, nor your loins unloosed; but be ready, for you know not the hour in which our Lord will come. But come together often, seeking the things which are befitting to your souls: for the whole time of your faith will not profit you, if you are not made perfect in the last time. For in the last days false prophets and corrupters shall be multiplied, and the sheep shall be turned into wolves, and love shall be turned into hate; for when lawlessness increases, they shall hate and persecute and betray one another, *and then shall appear the world-deceiver as Son of God, and shall do signs and wonders, and the earth shall be delivered into his hands, and he shall do iniquitous things which have never yet come to pass since the beginning. Then shall the creation of men come into the fire of trial, and many shall be made to stumble and shall perish; but those who endure in their faith shall be saved from under the curse itself.* And then shall appear the signs of the truth: first, the sign of an outspreading in heaven, then the sign of the sound of the trumpet. And third, the resurrection of the dead—yet not of all, but as it is said: "The Lord shall come and all His saints with Him." Then shall the world see the Lord coming upon the clouds of heaven.

E. Irenaeus (c. 120- c.202), *Against Heresies*

Chapter V. 26. In a still clearer light has John, in the Apocalypse, indicated to the Lord's disciples what shall happen in the last times, and concerning the ten kings who shall then arise, among whom the empire which now rules [the Earth] shall be partitioned. He teaches us what the ten horns shall be which were seen by Daniel, telling us that thus it had been said to him: "And the ten horns which thou sawest are ten kings, who have received no kingdom as yet, but shall receive power as if kings one hour with the beast. These have one mind, and give their strength and power to the beast. These shall make war with the Lamb, and the Lamb shall overcome them, because He is the Lord of lords and the King of kings." It is manifest, therefore, that of these [potentates], he who is to come shall slay three, and subject the remainder to his power, and that he shall be himself the eighth among them. And they shall lay Babylon waste, and burn her with fire, and shall give their kingdom to the beast, and put the Church to flight.

Chapter XXIX.1 And therefore, when in the end the Church shall be suddenly caught up from this, it is said, "here shall be tribulation such as has not been since the beginning, neither shall be." For this is the last contest of the righteous, in which, when they overcome, they are crowned with incorruption.

Chapter XXXV.1 For all these and other words were unquestionably spoken in reference *to the resurrection of the just, which takes place after the coming of Antichrist,* and the destruction of all nations under his rule; in [the times of] which [resurrection] the righteous shall reign in the earth.

Conclusion

The late George Ladd, a posttribulation rapture scholar and professor at Fuller Theological Seminary, made this observation concerning the writings of the church fathers of the early centuries after the apostles:

> The Antichrist was understood to be an evil ruler of the end-times who would persecute the church, afflicting her with great tribulation. Every church father who deals with the subject expects the church to suffer at the hands of the Antichrist. God would purify the church through suffering, and Christ would save her by His return at the end of the Tribulation… We can find no trace of pretribulationism in the early church; and no modern pretribulationist has successfully proved that this particular doctrine was held by any of the church fathers or students of the Word before the 19th century."[64]

Another posttribulation scholar echoed this sentiment:

> Although watching for the Lord's coming implies imminence to some people, it does not to the minds of others and did not so to the early church. — Robert Gundry[65]

Over the years, mid- or posttribulation teachers have done a great job in exposing the glaring weakness in the attempt use of the church fathers to support the rapture imminence doctrine. But prewrath rapture believers can confidently use the statements of the church fathers to identify the weaknesses of this position, while at the same time strengthening their own convictions about future rapture imminence. Consistent with the early fathers, prewrath holds that the church will be in the presence of the Antichrist and the great tribulation. Once that occurs, the rapture is finally imminent.

---

[64] Dr. George E. Ladd, *The Blessed Hope*, 31

[65] Robert Gundry, *The Church and the Tribulation,* 180.

APPENDIX 5

COSMIC DISTURBANCES: DARKNESS OF THE SUN, MOON, AND STARS

Unfortunately, the biblical concept of the darkening of the sun, the moon, and the stars, often referred to as "the cosmic disturbances," has not drawn much attention in influencing students of eschatology even though it is found multiple times in the Bible. It turns out to be a key expression that Robert Van Kampen researched and used to solve the puzzle of where the rapture should be properly located chronologically in relationship to the tribulation and the Day of the Lord. The first clue is found in Joel's prophecy:

> The Day of the Lord is near and it will come as destruction from the Almighty... there has never been anything like it nor will there be again after it... *the sun and the moon grow dark and the stars lose their brightness...* The day of the Lord is indeed great and very awesome and who can endure it? ... The *sun will be turned into darkness and the moon into blood, before the great and awesome day of the Lord comes... The sun and the moon grow dark and stars lose brightness* ... but the Lord is a refuge for His people and a stronghold to the sons of Israel." (Joel 1:15, 2:1-2, 10-11, 31, 3:15-16, emphasis added)

The critical thing that Joel reveals is the timing element with respect to the Day of the Lord and these cosmic disturbances. Notice that the prophet states they will take place *before* the Day of the Lord. Remember this as we now look at the words of Jesus regarding these same cosmic disturbances recorded in Matthew 24:29, Mark 13:24-25, and Luke 21:25. Matthew's account is in the context of the Lord answering the disciples' question, "What will be the sign of Your coming and of the end of the age?" (Matt. 24:3). Jesus proceeds to tell them many things (Matt. 24:4-28) that His followers are to watch for in advance of His coming during that terrible time (Matt. 24:9, 24:21). Now as we look closely and we see a second chronological clue associated with the same cosmic disturbances Joel previously mentioned:

> "But immediately *after* the tribulation of those days, *the sun will be darkened, and the moon will not give its light, and the stars will fall from the sky*, and the powers of the heavens will be shaken" (Matt. 24:29, emphasis added).

Now, if we combine the clear statements of both Joel and Jesus, we can create the following timeline by arranging the cosmic disturbances between the two bookend events they mentioned:

Tribulation ➤ Cosmic disturbances ➤ Day of the Lord

How can the tribulation be God's wrath, as pretribulation teachers claim, if the cosmic disturbances come *after* the one (the tribulation) but *before* the other, the Day of the Lord (God's wrath)? If a parent tells a child that he or she will attend elementary school *before* they go to middle school, then later explains *after* middle school they will go to high school, what do we logically conclude? The child cannot be in elementary and high school at the same time. They are different and separated chronologically by middle school. Likewise, the tribulation is also separated from the Day of the Lord by the cosmic disturbances, God's supernatural darkening of the universe.

Jesus then goes on to say:

> And then [after the tribulation of those days] the sign of the Son of Man will appear in the sky and then all the tribes of the earth will mourn and they will see

the Son of Man coming on the clouds of the sky with power and great glory. And He will send forth His angels with a great trumpet and they will *gather together His elect* from the four winds, from one end of the sky to the other. (Matt. 24:30-31, emphasis added)

The plain interpretation of this "gathering of the elect" is that it is the rapture taking place at the appearance of Jesus in the sky. Remember, He has been addressing His apostles as "you." This select group of Jewish men are Christians at this point, and they are the leaders of the followers of Christ, the church, made up of both Jews and Gentiles. Since they did not get raptured, some future generation of the church/elect will experience this gathering. They will go through that time period of great tribulation according to the teaching of Jesus on the Mount of Olives, but their removal means they will miss God's wrath, which will come upon God's enemies and not God's elect, the church. Pretribulation rapture teachers say this group of "the elect" is the nation of Israel at the end of Daniel's 70th Week as they are returned to their Promised Land. But this cannot be correct for three reasons. First is the close correspondence between Jesus' description of this gathering with Paul's description of the rapture in 1 Thessalonians 4:15-18. Note that Paul says the information he is discussing there comes "by the word of the Lord" (4:15) which most likely is the Olivet Discourse. In the contexts of both passages, there is an appearing or coming of Jesus in the sky, a gathering or catching up of the saints into the air, the presence of angels, and the sound of God's trumpet. In 1 Thessalonians, Paul gives the same details as Jesus gives to the apostles that night in the garden. Second, a word study on the word "elect" and its related words in the New Testament reveals that it is used exclusively to describe Christians, members of the church. The word "elect" is also found twice in the near context, Matthew 24:22 and 24:24, where it makes more sense that Jesus is referring to His "chosen ones," Christians, rather than to the nation of Israel. The days of the great tribulation will be shortened in order to save followers of Christ, not Israel (v. 22). The elect that are being tempted to be misled are Christians, not Israel (v. 24), because Israel has already been deceived, having signed the covenant with the Antichrist.

Third is the most significant. Let us examine the final time this expression about the "cosmic disturbances" is found in the New Testament. Read about the sixth seal John describes in the vision he received:

> And I looked when He broke the sixth seal, and there was a great earthquake; and *the sun became black as sackcloth made of hair, and the whole moon became like blood; and the stars of the sky fell to the earth,* as a fig tree casts its unripe figs when shaken by a great wind. And the sky was split apart like a scroll when it is rolled up, and every mountain and island were moved out of their places. And the kings of the earth and the great men and the commanders and the rich and the strong and every slave and free man hid themselves in the caves and among the rocks of the mountains; and they said to the mountains and to the rocks, "Fall on us and hide us from the presence of Him who sits on the throne, and from the wrath of the Lamb; *for the great day of their wrath has come,* and who is able to stand?" (Rev. 6:12-17, emphasis added)

The same extinguishing of the heavenly lights is mentioned here at the sixth seal. This once-in-the-history-of-the-world account recorded by John wholly agrees with what was described by Jesus as happening *after* the tribulation and by Joel 2:31 as taking place *before* the Day of the Lord. These simple and clear statements about the cosmic disturbances are a major support for the prewrath rapture and major problems for the pretribulation rapture. I have not found one teacher of the pretribulation rapture view who has dealt systematically with this issue of the Bible's timing related to these cosmic disturbances. Generally speaking, their answer is that they are spectacular and shocking phenomena which are just a part of God's wrath, which has been going on during the previous events of the Daniel's 70th Week. That cannot be true if one takes the words of Joel and Jesus, *before* and *after*, seriously. If you are a pretribulation rapture believer, I ask you to please do a study on these heavenly signs in both the Old and New Testaments.

Notice, too, that the sixth seal is immediately after the previous fifth seal, which portrays martyred Christians beneath God's throne. They were killed as a result of the hatred of the Antichrist and his campaign against anyone who rejects his rule during the first five seals. This is *his* wrath, not God's. Note this important detail, when these martyrs ask God:

> How long, O Lord, holy and true wilt Thou refrain
> from *judging and avenging our blood on those who*
> *dwell on the earth*? (Revelation 6:10 KJV, emphasis
> added)

If they are asking God why He is withholding judgment, the obvious implication is that *God's wrath has not yet begun.*

The period before the sixth seal is not God's wrath. The mention of cosmic disturbances at this time supports this critical point. The darkening of the world will allow the glorious appearance of Jesus at His second coming to be seen by everyone living at that time as Revelation 1:7 reveals: "Behold, He is coming with the clouds, and every eye will see Him, even those who pierced Him and all the tribes of the earth will mourn over Him."

APPENDIX 6

THE GAP THEORY: IS THERE TIME BETWEEN THE RAPTURE AND THE TRIBULATION?

Two different views exist dealing with the pretribulation rapture and the signing of the covenant between the Antichrist and Israel that begins the Day of the Lord. The first is what I will call the *traditional view*, which understands the rapture and the signing of the covenant as taking place simultaneously. This means that they happen at the same unpredictable time together, and the clock for the seven years of the 70th Week (which they also believe is God's wrath) begins ticking. Two teachers who represent this view wrote:

> This period [Day of the Lord] extends from Christ's coming "as a thief in the night" [the rapture] to the passing of the heavens and the earth that are now. — Dr. Lewis Sperry Chafer[66]

> The only way this day [Day of the Lord] could break unexpectedly upon the whole world is to have it begin immediately after the rapture of the church. It is thus concluded that the Day of the Lord is that extended period of time beginning with God's dealing with Israel after the rapture at the beginning

---

[66] Dr. L. S. Chafer, *Systematic Theology* (Dallas: Dallas Seminary Press), Volume VII, 110.

of the Tribulation period. —Dr. J. Dwight
Pentecost[67]

There is a second view held by other pretribulationists, which is that
after the "any moment" rapture takes place, a period of time will go
by before the covenant is signed and the tribulation/Daniel's 70th
Week begins. This position is what I call the *gap theory*. The
following two teachers represent this view (emphasis added):

> According to pretribulationists, the rapture of the
> church occurs at the end of the church age. It is
> followed by *a period of adjustment* in which a
> dictator and a ten-nation group emerge in the Middle
> East... this dictator enters into a treaty with Israel,
> indicated in Daniel 9:27 as intended to last for seven
> years. —John F Walvoord [68]

> The order of events is clear, the rapture will occur,
> and then the Antichrist will "be revealed."
> Remember, *the Seventieth Week does not begin at the
> time of the rapture. It will begin when the Antichrist
> signs the covenant* guaranteeing the peace of Israel
> for seven years. —Bob Shelton [69]

Although this gap theory was not emphasized at my time at Dallas
Seminary, I ran across it after I adopted the prewrath rapture
position. If I still believed in an "any moment," present-day rapture,
the gap theory camp of Walvoord and Shelton would be a
compelling alternative to the view of the traditionalists such as
Chafer and Pentecost. The reason is that it addresses an important
point in this book, which is that the world conditions are not yet in
place to allow for the events of the first half of the tribulation to start
happening at any moment right now (see Chapter 6, "The Problem
with Imminence Since 1967"). This unknown period, or gap of time,
allows for necessary changes on the world scene to occur. These

---

[67] Dr. J. Dwight Pentecost, *Things to Come*, 230-231.

[68] John F Walvoord, *The Blessed Hope and the Tribulation*, 132.

[69] Bob Shelton, *Prophecy in Context* (Greenville, SC: Bob Jones University Press,
2008), 60.

adjustments are required for the Antichrist to gain his worldwide influence and the events of Daniel's 70th Week to begin to occur.

Pretribulationists who hold to this theory leave us in the dark concerning how long this gap might be. We are not told whether it is days, or months, or years, but they all correctly acknowledge that it is logically necessary. However, this view creates a contradiction not only with the traditional pretribbers but also with Scripture. Remember, gap theorists claim the events of the seals, which make up the tribulation, are God's wrath. But their scenario of a delay of time denies the biblical principle that the wrath of God *will begin immediately after* the rescue of the righteous. In other words, the Scriptures do not allow for a time gap between the rapture and the start of God's wrath.

We find this principle in the biblical parallels with Noah and Lot (see Luke 17:26-30, Genesis 7:1-13; 19:12-29). In both of these instances, the righteous were first delivered by being taken away: Noah and his family escaped on the Ark, while Lot and his family were led out of the city by angels. Then, in both stories, immediately the wrath of God fell upon the unrighteous who remained behind. There was no indication of a gap of time for the unrighteous to continue on in their sin after the righteous had been separated from them. More specifically, Paul indicates that there is no time period separating the rapture and God's judgment (1 Thess. 4:13-5:3). It is universally accepted that 1 Thessalonians 4:13-19 indicates the rapture. (The chapter break must be ignored, since it is not inspired by the Holy Spirit.) This means the judgment of God's wrath follows immediately, as indicated by:

> Now as to the times and epochs, brethren, you have no need of anything to be written to you. For you yourselves know full well that the day of the Lord will come just like a thief in the night. While they are *saying "Peace and safety!"* then destruction will come upon them *suddenly* like birth pangs upon a woman with child, and they shall not escape. (1 Thessalonians 5:1-3, emphasis added)

This sudden unexpected coming and destruction is *upon the unbelieving*, not the true believers who have seen the signs and are patiently waiting for their deliverance. Being raptured allows them to escape completely from God's wrath. The rapture/escape and wrath/judgment are back to back. Teachers of the pretribulation gap theory have forced a non-biblical interpretation to accommodate their teaching of a present any moment rapture followed by the prophesied events of Daniel's 70th Week. The traditional, no gap position claims the rapture and covenant signing are simultaneous. Both of these pretribulation views have the same problem with the tribulation events of Daniel's 70th Week being able to unfold immediately if the rapture were to happen right now.

One other observation about the 1 Thessalonians 5:1-3 passage above concerns the phrase "while they are saying 'peace and safety.'" Some pretribulation rapture teachers contend that the actual condition of the world at the time of the any moment rapture is one of peace and safety. An example is Dave Hunt and the thesis in his book *Peace, Prosperity and the Coming Holocaust.* If this theory is true, and the world is living in a period of relative peace and safety when the rapture occurs, this would contradict any of the non-pretribulation rapture scenarios that teach that the rapture will take place at some time during the context of the tribulation. (See endnote *v* on p. 124 for more information about this subject) Each of the other three rapture positions hold that the rapture will occur under conditions that are anything but peace and safety. So, in the minds of pretribulationists, the mid-trib, post-trib, or prewrath raptures are not possible.

I believe pretribulationists are missing the meaning of what Paul is saying in the passage. Carefully note that the apostle writes: "While they are *saying* 'peace and safety . . .'" It does not say that peace and safety *actually exist* at that time. Rather, these are worldwide conditions for which the nations will be striving under the global leadership of the Antichrist and the false prophet. The goal of their campaign is to bring peace by means of a one-world economy, government, and religion (Rev. 13:3-8, 17:12-13). For them, this utopian end will come only if everyone will submit to their plan. But not everyone does, and that is what brings about the great tribulation upon those who refuse the mark of the beast. The proclaimers of "peace and safety" are unbelievers who have taken the mark and are trying to force these conditions upon the whole world. They will be shocked when their desire is brought to an abrupt end when Jesus stops the worldwide persecution by making His appearance in the sky, raptures the believers, and pours His Day-of-the-Lord wrath upon them (Matt. 24:15-42; Rev. 6:12-17; 2 Thess. 1:6-10).

APPENDIX 7

OTHER PREWRATH RESOURCES

Books

1. *The Prewrath Rapture of the Church,* by Marvin Rosenthal (Nashville: Thomas Nelson, 1990).
2. *The Rapture Question Answered: Plain and Simple,* by Robert Van Kampen (Grand Rapids: Fleming H. Revell, 1997).
3. *The Sign,* by Robert Van Kampen (Wheaton, Crossway Books, 1992)
4. *Antichrist Before the Day of the Lord,* by Dr. Alan Kurschner (Pompton Lakes, NJ: Eschatos Publishing, 2013)
5. *Silence in Heaven,* by Gordon Lawrence (Franklin, TN: Carpenter's Son Publishing, 2016)
6. *Before God's Wrath,* by H. L. Nigro (Bellefonte, PA: Strong Tower Publishing, 2004)
7. *Fight, Flight, or Faith,* by Charles Cooper (Bellefonte, PA: Strong Tower Publishing, 2008)

Websites

1. *EschatosMinistries.com* (Dr. Alan Kurschner)
2. *PrewrathRapture.com* (Charles Cooper)
3. *PrewrathMinistries.org* (Dr. Elbert Charpie)
4. *Strongtowerpublishing.com* (H. L. Nigro)
5. *BibleFragrances.com* (Ron Wallace)
6. *ChrisWhiteMinistries.com*
7. *ZionsHope.org*

YouTube Videos

1. Robert Van Kampen: *"The Biblical Defense of the Prewath Rapture"* (3 hours)
2. Charles Cooper: *"Interview on Prewrath Rapture"* (36 minutes)
3. Ron Wallace: *"The Day of the Lord; The Prewrath Rapture of the Church"* (2 hours)
4. Chris White: *"The Prewrath Rapture"* (2 hours)
5. Debate between Dr. Alan Kurschner and Dr. Thomas Ice (3 hours)

Although I may not agree with every detail of the positions of these individuals or organizations, there are two things we agree on. The first is that the rapture is not presently imminent before the tribulation events of Daniel's 70th Week and that the rapture is not the next biblical prophecy to be fulfilled. Secondly, we agree that the seals portion of the tribulation is not God's eschatological Day of the Lord's wrath, but the trumpets and the bowls are.

EPILOGUE

HOW TO KNOW THAT YOU WILL GO TO HEAVEN

The teachers of the various interpretations about the timing of the rapture may disagree about when it will take place. We are however, all in agreement of what is necessary to be included with the body of Christ that will someday be suddenly taken to be with the Lord. Do you know for sure if you will be included in the rapture and spend eternity in heaven experiencing unending joy, peace, and freedom? Or will you end up in the Lake of Fire, a place of conscience torment for having rejected God's provision for mankind's sins, Jesus' death on the cross. The greatest news you can ever hear is found in my favorite two passages in the Bible which sum up this gospel of God's love for us:

> For by grace you have been saved through faith; and that not of yourselves, it is the gift of God; not as a result of works, that no one should boast. (Ephesians 2:8-9)

> God has given us eternal life, and this life is in His Son. He who has the Son has the life; he who does not have the Son of God does not have the life. These things I have written to you who believe in the name of the Son of God, in order that

you may know that you have eternal life. (1 John 5:11-13):

Have you ever personally believed in Jesus Christ as your Savior? He died in our place experiencing God's wrath for everyone's sins, but it is only applied to those who receive it by means of their faith:

> But as many as received Him, to them He gave the right to become children of God, even to those who believe in His name... For God so loved the world, that He gave His only begotten Son, that whoever believes in Him should not perish, but have eternal life. (John 1:12; 3:16)

Let me illustrate this. Let us say there is a sporting event that is coming to your city and I go and purchase a ticket for every person living there and pass them out to everyone as free gifts from me. Every person who has a ticket will be permitted to go into the arena and enjoy the event, but they must do their part. If they show up and present the ticket then they will be allowed in without paying anything because I paid the full price for their admission. Those who have a ticket but do not come will miss the experience because for some reason there was something else more important, so they missed the benefits of my gracious gift. Likewise, it will be for those who refuse to receive the gift of eternal life that God offers to every person during their lifetime even though Jesus paid for their sins. They do not have God's righteousness so they will not be allowed to enter heaven.

At this point, let me ask you a very penetrating question. "If you were to die right now and God were to ask you, 'Why should I allow you into heaven?'. What would you say to Him?" If you respond by saying "I should be allowed into heaven because I did 'this' or 'that'. Essentially what you are saying is that you deserve to go to heaven because of your own works/self-righteousness. But this contradicts the truth of Ephesians 2:9 we saw earlier that says we cannot be saved by our works because it is a gift that must be received by faith in Jesus Christ. This leaves you in a pretty bad position before a holy and righteous God without a relationship with a savior.

If you are not sure if you have ever truly put your faith in Christ and know that you will spend eternity in heaven, you can settle that right now and begin this personal relationship with God. Most people have done this by simply having a heart to heart talk with God, that is what prayer is. If you do not know the words to say then maybe I can help you with words similar to what I said to Jesus when I trusted Him. I suggest that you first read these to make sure you understand them and know that they express what you want to do.

> Lord Jesus, although I do not deserve it, I am asking You for the forgiveness of my sins, would You please do that right now? Thank You for paying the price for my sins when You died on the cross, I want to receive You into my life by faith and I accept the gift of eternal life that You said I can have for free and can begin to experience right here and now. Thank You that You will do this because You are faithful to your Word. Amen

If you pray this prayer or something similar to it and you believe in Christ, then you can begin this new life with God. He promises that you can have the assurance of knowing you will end up in heaven for all eternity. This is found when Jesus said in John 5:24:

> Truly I say to you, he who hears My word and believes Him who sent me (God the Father) has eternal life, and does not come into judgment, but has passed out of death into life."

Also recall from God's word what I quoted earlier, "These things I have written to you who believe in the name of the Son of God, *in order that you may know that you have eternal life*" (1 John 5:13, emphasis added). If you have believed in Jesus Christ right now then you don't have to hope, think, or wish you have eternal life, the Bible says *you can know* you have eternal life this very moment! Maybe you feel different or maybe you do not feel different. It is important to understand that feelings come and go, but the Christian life is lived by believing in God's faithfulness to do what He has said in His Word and not our feelings. One of His great promises is: "I will never leave you or forsake you" (Hebrews 13:5). It is now important to begin to grow in faith and your knowledge of the Lord Jesus Christ. Find some other believers and join them in worship, and Bible study.

If perhaps you are not ready right now to take this step of believing in Jesus as your Savior and Lord, I want to encourage you to find someone you can talk to. Perhaps they can help you deal with the reason that is keeping you from receiving Christ's offer of eternal life. You are even welcome to contact me by email if you would like at TKeeley8@hotmail.com.